Pug

(from the American Kennel Club breed standard)

Tail: The tail is curled as tightly as possible over the hip. The double curl is perfection.

Body: The short back is level from the withers to the high tail set. The body is short and cobby, wide in chest and well ribbed up.

Hindquarters: The strong, powerful hindquarters have moderate bend of stifle and short hocks perpendicular to the ground. The hindquarters are in balance with the forequarters. The thighs and buttocks are full and muscular. Feet as in front.

Color: The colors are silver, apricot-fawn, or black. The silver or apricot-fawn colors should be decided so as to make the contrast complete between the color and the trace and the mask.

Pug

By Juliette Cunliffe

Contents

Training Your Pug

By Charlotte Schwartz
Be informed about the importance of training your Pug from the basics of housebreaking and understanding the development of a young dog to executing obedience commands (sit, stay, down, etc.).

Health Care of Your Pug

Discover how to select a qualified vet and care for your dog at all stages of life. Topics include vaccinations, skin problems, dealing with external and internal parasites and common medical and behavioral conditions, with a special section on eye disease.

Showing Your Pug

Enter the dog show world and find out how dog shows work and how a champion is made. Go beyond the conformation ring to other types of competitive events.

KENNEL CLUB BOOKS® PUG
ISBN: 978-1-59378-268-9

Copyright © 2003, **2008** • Kennel Club Books® • A Division of BowTie, Inc.
40 Broad Street, Freehold, NJ 07728 USA
Cover Design Patented: US 6,435,559 B2 • Printed in South Korea

10 9 8 7 6

Photography by Mary Bloom, Isabelle Français and Carol Ann Johnson, with additional photos provided by: Norvia Behling, T. J. Calhoun, Carolina Biological Supply, Doskocil, James Hayden-Yoav, James R. Hayden, RBP, Bill Jonas, Dwight R. Kuhn, Dr. Dennis Kunkel, Mikki Pet Products, Antonio Philippe, Phototake, Jean Claude Revy, Dr. Andrew Spielman and Alice van Kempen.

Illustrations by Renée Low.

The publisher wishes to thank Pat Withers and the rest of the owners of dogs featured in this book.

Whether you believe the Pug is Chinese, Dutch or Greek, and whether you call the breed Pug, Mops or Carlin, you will concur that this is a most fascinating and worthy choice as a pet dog.

HISTORY OF THE
PUG

Theories about the origin of the Pug have caused much debate over the years, some thinking the breed to have developed in the Far East, others thinking it developed in Europe. It is now generally accepted that the Pug originated in China, from where it spread to Japan and later to Europe. It is also highly probable that the short-nosed Pug, crossed with other longer-faced European breeds, lies behind many of the other shorter-headed breeds.

In China there has long been a breed of dog known as the Happa (sometimes spelled Ha-pa), which is similar to a smooth-coated Pekingese. Indeed, many people believe that the Happa may be the progenitor of the Pug. Short-mouthed dogs in China are known as Lo-sze, and although they may well have been known there as far back as 1115 BC, there is no record of them until 663 BC. The Lo-sze had clear features distinguishing it from the Pekingese: the muzzle was different, the coat was short and the ears were small and vine-shaped. By 732 AD we read of a small short-faced dog, known as the Suchuan pai dog, that was among gifts sent from Korea to Japan.

THE NAME "PUG"

The word "Pai" came to be used as the name for this type of dog, and it is possible that to Western ears this name may have resembled the name now used in the West, "Pug." In 1731 the word "pug" was defined in a dictionary as a nickname for a monkey or dog. Marmosets were popular as pets at that time, and the Pug's squashed-in face probably caused it to share the same name.

Another possibility is that the name originated from the Latin word *pugnus*, which means fist, as some people thought that the shape of the Pug's face resembled a clenched fist. The word "pug" or "pugge" was also a term of endearment, though it may also be a derivation of "Puck," conjuring up Shakespearean images of an impish face.

In some Continental countries, the Pug is still known by the rather quaint name "Mops," which comes from the Dutch word *Mopshund*. The verb *mopperen* means to grumble, and the name "Mops" may well have come into use because of the breed's wrinkled, frowning appearance.

In France the name used was Carlin, after a famous 18th-century actor who was renowned for his role as Harlequin. It is thought that the name Carlin was, and still is, used for the Pug in France because of the breed's black mask.

THE BREED IN CHINA

In China, dogs were frequently treated almost like royalty, even with titles of rank being bestowed upon some of them. They were carefully guarded, and many had servants employed to care for them and to see that they enjoyed every comfort. Understandably, the Pug was owned primarily by those within Court circles or from the ruling classes of the country, and often the dogs were treated primarily as ornaments.

The Pug enjoyed great popularity in China at least until the 12th century, but from then on interest appeared to wane and there was little mention of the breed until early in the 16th century.

THE PUG COMES WEST

It is now generally accepted that the Pug originated in the Orient and eventually appeared in Europe, much resembling the breed known there today. Many people believe that the Pug descended from the mastiff breeds, with ancestors such as the fighting dogs of ancient

Since arriving to the West, the Pug has changed considerably in conformation. This modern Pug is posing with a Victorian plaster model that may reveal some of the Continental crosses to Bulldogs.

Like the Pug, the Shih Tzu, another Chinese breed, once found favor with royalty around the world and today is counted among the world's most popular toy breeds.

Greece. Certainly in Europe there were some extraordinary cross-matings in years gone by—with the Bulldog, among others—but in China the aim was certainly to breed dogs as true to type as possible. It is these that formed a firm foundation for today's Pug.

Before reaching the West, the Pug was popular throughout Asia and it seems to have wended its way to Europe via Russia. The aunt of Russia's Catherine the Great was reputed to have kept a score of Pugs and the same number of parrots in a single room. Perhaps equally fascinating is the picture conjured up in our minds when we learn that several of this Princess's dogs always accompanied her to church.

A very successful Pug from the 1930s' dog show world of Britain was Miss F. M. Daniel's Eng. Ch. Bouji, bred from Eng. Ch. Pouf-pouf.

The Pug has been very much connected with Holland, for it has been very popular there, though in the early years they were known as "Dutch Mastiffs." This name may help explain the

confusion that arose over the breed's origin. Pugs from Holland were certainly destined to have a great influence on the spread of the breed throughout Europe.

The Dutch East India Company played an important role in trade with the Orient. It is clear that on many of the ships' return journeys, both Pugs and Pekingese were brought back as precious cargo. It is a Pug that is reputed to have saved the life of William the Silent when, at Hermigny, around 1572, the Prince was under surprise attack from Spanish troops. When the Pug heard the noise of the troops he made a great noise, scratching and crying, and leapt upon the

face of the Prince to awaken him. From then on, the Prince always kept such a dog, and, subsequently, Pugs were the favorite breed at the Dutch Court.

THE PUG GOES TO ENGLAND

The grandson of William the Silent was William of Orange who went to England with his wife, Mary, in 1688 to take the throne. With the couple came many Pugs, each wearing an orange ribbon around its neck to denote its connection to the Royal House of Orange. The breed quickly found favor in England, where it soon became known as the Dutch Pug, although later Pug or Pug-dog

was the name used.

In 18th-century Britain, the Pug became highly fashionable, not only at court but also among people of "quality." Indeed when ladies ventured outdoors, it was quite "the done thing" for them

The long-haired wonder we know as the Pekingese is regarded as similar to the short-haired Happa dog, known in China. In appearance, the Happa differs from the Pekingese in coat, ears and muzzle.

In the 1920s the famed dog caricaturist, Scott Langley, depicted these dogs in a sketch he called "Pug Dogs."

The decline of the Pug was by no means averted by the author Taplin, who wrote of the Pug, "...applicable to no sport, appropriated to no useful purpose, susceptible of no predominant passion..." Such comments could surely not have served to enhance the popularity of the breed that all too quickly became known, rather contemptuously, as an "old lady's pet."

But the Pug did not remain out of favor for long, thanks in part to Queen Victoria, who was such an ardent dog lover and who owned Pugs among several other breeds. It is likely that her earliest Pugs were given to her by royal relations on the Continent. Her dogs appear to have been kept as nursery dogs, most appropriate for this breed that gets along so well with children.

The Prince of Wales gave a Pug named Bully to his wife, Queen Alexandra, before leaving for an Indian tour. Of course, Queen Alexandra, too, was

(Top photo) Eng. Ch. Princess Pretty, owned by Lord Wrottesley, was bred in 1920 by Miss Spurling. (Lower photo) Eng. Ch. Penella of Inver was bred in 1927 by Miss M. D. Hatrick.

to be accompanied by a turbaned servant and a Pug. Charlotte, wife of George III (1760–1820), was also inordinately fond of the breed and had many, one of which is depicted in a painting hanging in Hampton Court. However, by the end of the reign of George IV in 1830, the Pug was no longer fashionable and by the middle of the 19th century had fallen into decline.

TOP HAT

China's Emperor Ling Ti (168–190 AD) was so fond of his little dog that it was honored with the official hat and belt of the Chin Hsien grade. This poor little dog must have looked most extraordinary wearing this enormous hat. It measured over 8 inches high at front, nearly 4 inches high behind and 10 inches wide!

NURSING PUGS
According to Hester Lynch Piozzi, friend of Dr. Johnson, Pug puppies were often weaned on the breasts of their owners' servants. The writer seems not to have liked this idea at all!

famous for her devotion to dogs and took an active interest in dog shows, an increasingly popular activity, particularly among Pug owners.

There were two main strains in Britain in the early decades of the 19th century. A publican by the name of Mr. Morrison bred pale fawn Pugs in Waltham Green, and Lord and Lady Willoughby d'Eresby used imported blood to improve type. There is some conjecture as to whether the d'Eresbys actually obtained two Pugs from a Russian tightrope walker, or whether they got a dog from a Hungarian countess who lived in Vienna. Nevertheless, the Willoughby Pugs, and indeed the Morrison Pugs, played a very important part in the breed's early development in Britain. It has been suggested that dogs of the Willoughby kennel came directly from the Royal kennels of Queen Charlotte. In time the two strains came together and so, to a certain extent, lost their individuality, though even today

From Vero Shaw's *Book of the Dog,* published in 1881, we find this excellent painting by C. Burton Parker, depicting a Yorkshire Terrier, an Italian Greyhound and a Pug.

This charming
photograph from
the 1930s shows a
Pug lover with an
armful of brindle
and black Pug
puppies.

the distinctive bloodlines show through occasionally.

Although their story does not necessarily have foundation, the apricot-fawn-colored Pugs, Lamb and Moss, also feature prominently in breed history. Their parents apparently were captured during the siege of the Summer Palace in China in the 1860s and supposedly were brought to England by the Marquis of Wellesley, where they were given to a lady named Mrs. St. John. This may not be exactly true, as various facts do not quite agree with history, but these two

This charming photograph from the 1930s shows a Pug lover with an armful of brindle and black Pug puppies.

A modern British
Pug poses with a
toy wooden Pug
from the
Victorian era, a
time when the
Pug was
immensely
popular.

dogs were certainly the parents of Click, one of the most important Pugs in the breed's history. He was an invaluable stud, producing some very good bitches, and he also had a great bearing on the breed in the USA.

BLACK PUGS

In 1877 black was considered a "new" color in the breed. Again there has always been debate as to the actual origin of Lady Brassey's black Pugs, but she certainly exhibited some black ones at Britain's Maidstone Show in 1886. One of these was Jack Spratt, who possibly may have been acquired by Lady Brassey on her short trip to China.

However, although black was then claimed as a new color, we know from the paintings of William Hogarth that blacks existed before then. Hogarth's *House of Cards*, painted in 1730, depicts a black Pug. A hundred

years later, Queen Victoria owned a black Pug that was marked with white. The latter, though, may have been brought into England, perhaps as a gift to the Queen from China.

It has been said that black Pugs had been bred for many years earlier in England, but because they had been bred from apricot-fawns they were considered mutations and thus destroyed at birth. It is also possible, however, that such "blacks" were not true blacks (ebonies), but instead were smuts, so were not considered attractive.

Black Pugs today are considered acceptable and desirable. In times gone by, the black coat color was frowned upon.

A contemporary Pug painting on an old theme by the talented artist Diedre Ashdown. (Courtesy of the artist.)

Eng. Ch. Dark Diamond in 1930 represents a typical British champion black Pug.

Eng. Chs. Peter and Paul won 14 Challenge Certificates in the 1930s.

Eng. Ch. Paul of Inver was a great winner until he was killed in an accident when he was four years old.

Jan, owned by Miss Voy, was the son of Eng. Ch. Scaramouche of Broadway, bred by Mrs. Powers.

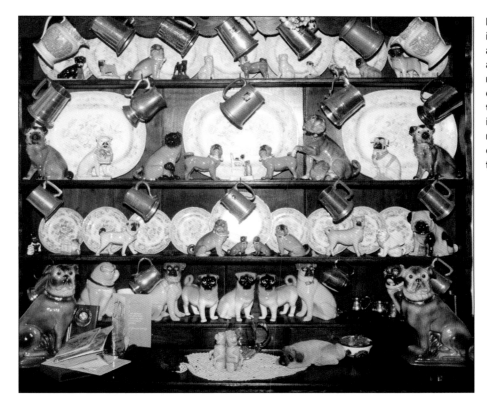

Pugs are immensely collectable. Many owners adopt two or more Pugs and often decorate their homes with invaluable memorabilia celebrating their favorite topic.

In 1896 efforts were made to show the black Pug as an English-made variety, but despite considerable support this was not allowed. There was a very well-known black Pug who was known as the "singing Pug." Apparently, when given a chord on the piano, or by humming, he could pick up the note and sing most tunefully. The black Pug certainly had its admirers, and in 1900 two were reported as having been sold to fanciers in New York for a sum totaling £350.

CRUFT AND THE PUG

The formation of Britain's first Pug Dog Club was discussed in 1881 and approved by The Kennel Club in January 1883. Although not the club's first Secretary, Mr. Charles Cruft at one time held this office. In 1885 the club held its first show and the show of 1887 was promoted by Cruft himself, revealing his prowess as an organizer of such events. Of course, Cruft went on to produce England's most prestigious dog shows, which were resumed by The Kennel Club itself in 1948.

THE PUG IN ART

Many artists have incorporated the charming little Pug in their paintings, and from these paintings we have a good indication of the quality of dogs at the time. Goya portrayed some lovely examples of the breed, and from these we can tell that the quality of the breed in Spain was high.

William Hogarth (1697–1764) owned a Pug; his *Self Portrait* is well known, depicting the artist with his dog. He also included Pugs in other portraits and conversation pieces.

Reinagle is another artist, renowned as an animal painter, who portrayed the charming Pug in his work. Many early dog books include engravings of this adorable breed, though not all of these engravings have been well thought of by breed enthusiasts. Although there are many other portrayals of note, *Blonde and Brunette*, painted by Charles Burton Barber in 1879, is one of my favorites, depicting a young lady engrossed in her book while her Pug rests comfortably in her arm.

Meissen, or Dresden, porcelain is also famed for its portrayal of the Pug. Indeed, the Pug must surely rank among one of the most popular breeds of dog portrayed in porcelain and other collectable items. Most of those from the 18th century fetch very

A litter from the 1930s bred by Miss Voy, representing the second generation from famed breeding pair Eng. Ch. Miss Penelope and Dandy Dicker of Baronshalt.

high prices, and even those from the 19th century are increasingly scarce. Sometimes such renderings are discovered of Pugs with cropped ears, and many have bells around their collars, making them even more charming.

THE PUG COMES TO AMERICA
Although we lack documentation on the arrival of the first Pugs to America, we do know that some dogs were in the country shortly after the Civil War. The breed gained attention because of its uniqueness and, during the 1880s, many Pugs were shown. The breed gained recognition from the American Kennel Club (AKC) in 1885 and was classified in the Toy Group, as it is in other countries around the world.

The breed fell into relative obscurity at the turn of the 20th century as other breeds gained favor, many of which were "exotic imports" at the time. Breeders on the East Coast began stirring up interest in the Pug again, and by 1931 a club was formed. Twenty

William Hogarth's famous *Self Portrait* with his dog, painted about 1740, may be the most celebrated of all Pug renderings.

JOSEPHINE'S "FORTUNE"
A Pug by the name of Fortune belonged to Napoleon Bonaparte's first wife, Josephine. Fortune was reputed to have had a somewhat possessive nature, and when the dwarfish man who was to become Emperor entered the bedchamber on his wedding night, the dwarfish dog promptly bit him!

years later, the Pug Dog Club of America (PDCA), the current parent club for the Pug, was established as the breed's principal promoter and protector in the US. The first members of the PDCA were prominent Pug people such as Dr. Nancy Riser, Filomena Doherty, Mrs. Joseph

Rowe, Suzanne Bellinger, Dr. James Stubbs, Ralph Adair, Mary Lou Mann, Miriam Dock, Mr. and Mrs. John Madore and J. Hartley Mellick, Jr.

By the 1940s, Pug breeders began producing consistent winners. Such kennels as Catawba, Winna Pugs, Paramount, Gin Rickey, Lucky Ace, Clavone and others began to dominate the show scene in North America. The following decade, breeders such as Filomena Doherty, Frederic Soderberg, Mrs. Edwin Pickhardt, Gordon Winders and Rolla Blaylock produced top winners, including an early Best in Show winner, Ch. Pugholm Peter Punkin Eater. To add to the growing Pug fraternity, Peter and Carolyn Standish, Ann Crowley, Shirley and Rayne Thomas, Esther and Gus Wolf, Hazel Martens, Barbara Minella and Agnes Miner represent just some of the important breeders responsible for the Pug's climb to fame in the US in the 1960s and 1970s.

Since those decades, the Pug has remained a popular breed, frequently seen in the show ring and counted among the top 20 breeds according the AKC's registration statistics. Although the Pug is not as flashy and intense as other top contenders in the Toy Group, including his relatives, the Pekingese and Shih Tzu, the breed does well in conformation shows and has

racked up an impressive number of Best in Show awards over the years. In 1981, the first Pug ever to win the famous Westminster Kennel Club Show was named Ch. Dhandys Favorite Wood-chuck, owned by Robert A. Hauslohner. To date, "Chucky," as his friends called him, is the only Pug to receive this great honor. He was bred by Mrs. W. U. Braley and Mrs. R. D. Hutchinson and was handled to the win by Robert Barlow.

The Pug's popularity continues to grow and there are quality specimens in most countries around the world. This handsome Pug was photographed in the Netherlands, a country with which the breed has strong ties.

CHARACTERISTICS OF THE

PUG

Described by some breed enthusiasts as "the perfect blend of dog appeal and wistfulness," a Pug will readily keep his owners amused and entertained for hours on end with his clown-like personality. Ownership of Pugs often runs in human families, with several generations having happily owned the breed. This is a personality dog, one just as comfortable living in a small home as he is in a spacious one. Some Pug dog owners call their Pugs "little people," and, when you know the breed, it is easy to understand why!

Pugs are fairly odor-free, so much so that the family cat doesn't even mind sharing a cat nap with the Pug, if he's also well mannered.

The Pug's bark is a surprisingly deep one for the breed's size. Indeed, a Pug is usually rather a good watchdog, ready to bark when the doorbell rings or when someone approaches the house. If you are a light sleeper, it might also be worth bearing in mind that although not all Pugs snore, many do!

An exceptionally clean little dog, the Pug is remarkably free from doggy odors. Some consider the Pug a very suitable breed for elderly and disabled people, though you should not forget that Pugs, like all other dogs, require some exercise. All things considered, a Pug usually seems happy to be whatever his owners need. He can be content to roll up in a ball at your feet while you are knitting or watching TV, he will enjoy a lively ball game or he can just be a friendly clown, providing entertainment for his audience at home.

Although the origin of the breed lies in China, the Pug differs considerably in personality from many other breeds from the Far East in that he does not display the usual reserved air of superiority. The Pug is a unique breed in many ways and has numerous admirers, in part because of his puckish sense of humor and irresistible, engaging ways.

PHYSICAL CHARACTERISTICS
Small, squarely built and cobby, the Pug has well-knit proportions and a certain hardness of muscle, making him a strong little animal and quite different from the majority of breeds falling into the Toy Group. Ideal weight is 14–18 lbs, but certainly some are rather heavier, and there are probably few males weighing under 18 lbs. Although the breed standard does not differentiate between the size of dogs and bitches, generally Pug dogs are somewhat larger than their female counterparts.

You should always remember that Pugs usually enjoy their food and might be considered rather greedy. Hence, it is necessary to keep strict control of your Pug's diet so that the dog does not become overweight. Once a Pug has reached the stage when he carries too much weight, it is extremely difficult to get the weight off again!

The chest of the Pug is wide and the body is set on strong legs. The large, round, wrinkled head with dark, globular eyes is offset at the rear by a high-set tail, curled tightly over the hip, with a double curl being highly desirable.

TAKING CARE
Science is showing that as people take care of their pets, the pets are taking care of their owners. A recent study published in the *American Journal of Cardiology* found that having a pet can prolong his owner's life. Pet owners generally have lower blood pressure, and pets help their owners to relax and keep more physically fit. It was also found that pets help to keep the elderly connected to their communities.

COLORS AND COAT

Pugs are found in silver, apricot-fawn and black, although presently silvers are few and far between. Although not mentioned in the breed standard, apricot-fawn and silver Pugs have a double coat, which consists of an outer weather-resistant coat and a softer, insulating undercoat. Black Pugs have a single coat.

Colors are clearly defined and should have a black line extending from the back of the head along the top of the back to the twist of the tail, called a trace. The mask (or muzzle) should be as black as possible, as should the ears, moles on cheeks and the diamond or "thumb mark" on the dog's forehead.

Many breeders consider the overall quality of today's black Pugs to be not as good as once it was. However, there is still a handful of top-quality black specimens that are well capable of holding their own with the best, comparing favorably with those of years gone by. Unfortunately, today there are only very few breeders currently specializing in blacks. It is hard to breed good blacks, for the coat should be jet black and no other markings should be visible. Because of the color, the desired wrinkles on the head need to be deep and clear in order to be seen.

The Pug's coat is easy to maintain, for it is fine, smooth and soft. This is a short, glossy coat that should be neither harsh to the touch nor woolly. Pugs' coats do shed to a certain extent, though not so much as those of many other breeds. People with sensitive allergies ought to check before buying a Pug that the coat does not affect them. You must always keep foremost in mind that a dog should remain with you for life, so you must be certain that you are making a well-informed decision before deciding upon a particular breed.

On the subject of allergies, some Pugs themselves suffer from flea allergies, so it is extra-important to keep your Pug free from parasites.

Because of the wrinkling on the head of the Pug, special care needs to be taken to keep this area clean, so as to avoid

WHAT A CHARMING SIGHT!

Years ago in Italy the Pug could be seen wearing strikingly colorful and well-cut jackets, often with pants. Soon the breed came to be looked upon contemptuously, although looking back today you can imagine what a charming sight these colorful little canines made!

any build-up that can cause irritation to the skin.

TAILS
The Pug's twisted tail is natural and is not cropped to look this way. In fact, the tail is not so short as you might think at first glance—it is just that it is very well curled.

It has recently been realized that a few Pugs suffer from a vertebral problem, seemingly because of the curled tail. This is usually noticed before the age of 12 months and can unfortunately cause a dog to be crippled.

PERSONALITY
This is a breed with great charm, dignity and intelligence, though, like other intelligent breeds, he can be rather self-willed. The Pug is an even-tempered breed with a happy, lively disposition. The friendship displayed is often effusive; indeed, most Pugs seem constantly delighted to meet people and show special

A male and female Pug (notice the difference in size) get along quite well in the same household.

affection to children. However, although the Pug shows friendliness toward strangers, it is to his owner and family that he is most devoted.

The Pug is a fearless breed that, despite his diminutive size, enjoys exercise outdoors and has something of a brave, sporting instinct that can occasionally cause him to run into trouble with other dogs. That is not to say that Pugs are generally aggressive, though they might appear so sometimes because of jealousy.

Inside the home, the Pug likes nothing more than warmth and comfort, with general affection and petting bestowed on him by his owners.

"Getting to know you" the toy-dog way, as this Pug makes the acquaintance of a Yorkshire Terrier friend.

Pugs and children
can spend many
happy hours
together;
however, children
should always be
supervised when
spending time
with dogs.

PUGS AND CHILDREN

Pugs certainly seem happy in the company of children, and usually the feeling is mutual. This is a breed that always seems ready for a bit of "rough and tumble" but, when in the company of dogs, children should always be supervised by adults. If children are taught to respect dogs, both they and the

Pugs involved can spend many happy hours in each other's company. Nevertheless, adults should never allow either to become over-excited.

HEALTH CONSIDERATIONS

Because of the Pug's short foreface, the breed can suffer breathing difficulties and does not easily tolerate extreme heat. In general, though, the Pug is a reasonably healthy breed and can live until a ripe old age. It is, however, worth bearing in mind that often Pugs do not take well to anesthesia, so it is important to mention this to your vet if an operation is pending.

Pugs, like other short-nosed (brachycephalic) breeds, can be prone to elongation of the soft palate. The Pug has been bred for centuries to have a short nose and wrinkled skin; as a result, the soft palate tends to be wide and flabby. As the dog pants, the soft palate gets drawn back into the larynx so that air is unable to enter the lungs. It is this that causes Pugs to suffer distress in unusually hot weather or following exertion.

CORRECTIVE SURGERY

Surgery is often used to correct genetic bone diseases in dogs. Usually the problems present themselves early in the dog's life and must be treated before bone growth stops.

It is therefore necessary to keep a very careful eye on your Pug in hot weather and always to be on the lookout for any sign of fatigue during exercise. Danger signs are protruding, staring eyes and the head's being held high in an effort to draw in more air. A dog can lose consciousness and his breathing may stop, but sometimes will resume within only a few seconds, though not always.

It goes without saying that any dog can suffer distress and can die if left in a car on a warm day, even with ventilation. Pugs are even more likely to be affected than the majority of other breeds, so beware! Never leave your Pug in your car, and this tragedy will be avoided.

Should your dog be unfortunate enough to suffer from heat exhaustion, cold water or ice should be put on the head, face and body immediately; the dog should also be kept as cool and quiet as possible. Any Pug that seems particularly prone to the consequences of an elongated soft palate should certainly not be bred from.

Here it is worth mentioning that, whether or not your Pug has breathing problems, as with any other breed, food should never be given immediately before or following strenuous exercise. Opinions vary, but when exercising my own dogs I

DOGS, DOGS, GOOD FOR YOUR HEART!
People usually purchase dogs for companionship, but studies show that dogs can help to improve their owners' health and level of activity, as well as lower a human's risk of coronary heart disease. Without even realizing it, when a person puts time into exercising, grooming and feeding a dog, he also puts more time into his own personal health care. Dog owners establish more routine schedules for their dogs to follow, which can have positive effects on a their own health. Dogs also teach us patience, offer unconditional love and provide the joy of having a furry friend to pet!

always like to allow one full hour's rest before or after any meal.

A Pug should have eyes that are gloriously described as globular in shape, but they should not be too bulbous. This shape can bring with it various problems in that the eyes, being prominent, are more likely to be exposed to injury or to become damaged through dust and dirt becoming entrapped. Sensible Pug owners ensure that there are no rose bushes with thorns or any other spiky plants in their gardens.

At any sign of injury to the eye, veterinary attention should be sought, but, in an emergency, a couple of drops of very slightly warmed castor oil can be soothing. If a Pug has suffered a cold in the eye, the eye may be bathed either with warm milk or with cold tea. If ever a Pug's eye is watering, this is a sign that something is amiss and the cause should be investigated without delay to avoid long-term damage.

Pigmentary keratitis, often indicated by the dog's rubbing his eyes, can lead to blindness. The condition is linked to poor tear production, entropion and dry eye. Entropion involves one or more eyelids' turning inward, so that they touch the eyeball. In consequence, this causes irritation to the cornea and can be painful. Entropion can involve in-turning eyelashes, but in a wrinkled breed such as the Pug, it can also occur in a mild form if a dog loses weight suddenly. At any sign of entropion, whatever the suspected cause, veterinary attention should be sought.

Luxating patella is a dislocation of the kneecap, caused because the kneecap of an affected dog has a shallow groove. This is a hereditary defect and is known in Pugs.

Another problem that has affected the Pug is one normally associated with larger breeds. This is hip dysplasia, in which the ball and socket joint of the hip fit badly, causing consequent lameness and discomfort. Fortunately, hip dysplasia is not now so prevalent in the breed as it was in earlier years. Dogs with poor hips or luxating patellas should not be used in breeding programs.

GENERAL GOOD HEALTH AT HOME

A Pug's anal glands can cause problems if not evacuated periodically. In the wild, anal glands are cleared regularly to set the dog's mark, but in domestic dogs this function is no longer necessary; thus, their contents can build up and clog, causing discomfort. Anal glands on either side of the anus that need emptying are usually noticed if a Pug drags its rear end along the ground or keeps turning around to attend to the uncomfortable patch.

While care must be taken not to cause injury, anal glands can be evacuated by pressing gently on either side of the anal opening and by using a piece of cotton or a tissue to collect the foul-smelling matter. If anal glands are allowed to become impacted, abscesses can form, causing pain and the need for veterinary attention.

Pugs can get into all sorts of mischief, so it is not unknown for them to inadvertently swallow something poisonous in the course of their investigations. Obviously an urgent visit to your vet is required under such circumstances, but if possible, when you telephone him, you should advise which poisonous substance has been ingested, as different treatments are needed. Should it be necessary to cause your dog to vomit (which is not always the case with poisoning), a small lump of baking soda, given orally, will have an immediate effect. Alternatively, a small teaspoonful of salt or mustard, dissolved in water, will have a similar effect but may be more difficult to administer and not as quick in its action.

Fits in Pug puppies while they are teething are not unknown. These are not usually serious and are fleetingly brief, caused only by the pain of

SKIN PROBLEMS
Eczema and dermatitis are skin problems that occur in many breeds, and they often can be tricky problems to solve. Frequently bathing the dog will remove skin oils and will cause the problem to worsen. Allergies to food or to something in the environment can also cause the problem. Consider trying homeopathic remedies in addition to seeing your veterinarian for direction.

teething. Of course you must be certain that the cause is not more serious, but giving a puppy something hard on which to chew will usually solve this temporary problem.

PUG

The breed standard for the Pug is set down by the Pug Dog Club of America, approved by the American Kennel Club and revised occasionally by the parent club.

A breed standard is designed effectively to paint a picture in words, though each reader will almost certainly have a slightly different way of interpreting these words. However, reading the words alone is never enough to fully comprehend the intricacies of a breed. In addition, it is necessary for Pug devotees to watch other Pugs being judged at shows and, if possible, to attend breed seminars, thus enabling them to absorb as much as possible about the breed they love so much.

Breed standards vary slightly from country to country, so judges, when officiating outside the USA, should always aim to assess the dogs in relation to the standard of the country concerned.

Each AKC standard commences with a short section under the heading "General Appearance" that gives a short *précis* of what the breed should look like. From this opening sentence, you can see immediately that a typical Pug should be decidely square and cobby; therefore, an excessively long-legged or long-backed Pug would be untypical of the breed.

It is generally accepted that it is not necessary for a judge to peer inside a Pug's mouth, merely to feel the shape of the jaw and to look at the expression created. However, the standard does state that the mouth is to be very slightly undershot. This means that, although they should not show, the lower teeth protrude

SQUARE AND COBBY

The general appearance of the Pug is square and cobby, described in Latin as *multum in parvo*, relating to the breed's compactness and meaning "a lot in a small space."

ever so slightly more than the upper ones, giving the desired expression. From this we can see that understanding the meaning of the words written in the standard is important.

However familiar one is with the breed, it is always worth refreshing one's memory by re-reading the standard, for it is sometimes too easy to conveniently forget certain features of the breed, such as that the nails on a Pug should be black.

The standard undoubtedly helps breeders to breed stock that comes as close to the standard as possible and helps judges to know exactly what they are looking for in choosing as typical a Pug as possible to head their line of winners.

THE AMERICAN KENNEL CLUB STANDARD FOR THE PUG

General Appearance: Symmetry and general appearance are

Ribbons are awarded at dog shows to the dogs that most closely conform to their breed standard. This young man has had a successful day showing his handsome Pug.

decidedly square and cobby. A lean, leggy Pug and a dog with short legs and a long body are equally objectionable.

Size, Proportion, Substance: The Pug should be *multum in parvo,* and this condensation (if the word may be used) is shown by compactness of form, well knit proportions, and hardness of developed muscle. Weight from 14 to 18 pounds (dog or bitch) desirable. Proportion square.

SELECTIVE BREEDING

It was once thought that the Pug's short face came about because puppies' nasal bones were deliberately crushed. However, this is a fallacy. This breed's shortened foreface has been developed through centuries of selective breeding.

Head: The head is large, massive, round—not apple-headed, with no indentation of the skull. The eyes are dark in color, very large, bold and prominent, globular in shape, soft and solicitous in expression, very lustrous, and, when excited, full of fire. The ears are thin, small, soft, like black velvet. There are two kinds—the "rose" and the "button." Preference is given to the latter. The wrinkles are large and deep. The muzzle is short, blunt, square, but not upfaced. Bite: A Pug's bite should be very slightly undershot.

Neck, Topline, Body: The neck is slightly arched. It is strong, thick and with enough length to carry the head proudly. The short back is level from the withers to the high tail set. The body is short and cobby, wide in chest and well ribbed up. The tail is curled as tightly as possible over the hip. The double curl is perfection.

Forequarters: The legs are very strong, straight, of moderate length, and are set well under. The elbows should be directly under the withers when viewed from the side. The shoulders are moderately laid back. The pasterns are strong, neither steep nor down. The feet are neither so long as the foot of the hare, nor so round as that of the cat; well split-up toes, and the nails black. Dewclaws are generally removed.

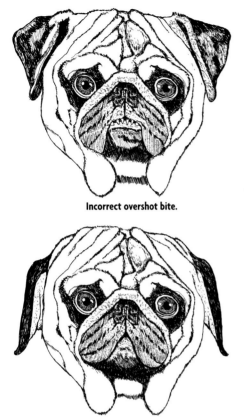

Incorrect overshot bite.

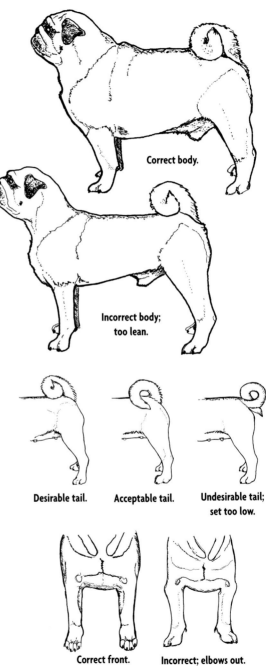

Correct body.

Incorrect ears; set too low and too long.

Incorrect body;
too lean.

Desirable tail. Acceptable tail. Undesirable tail;
set too low.

Correct head and "button" ears.

Correct front. Incorrect; elbows out.

Hindquarters: The strong, powerful hindquarters have moderate bend of stifle and short hocks perpendicular to the ground. The legs are parallel when viewed from behind. The hindquarters are in balance with the forequarters. The thighs and buttocks are full and muscular. Feet as in front.

Coat: The coat is fine, smooth, soft, short and glossy, neither hard nor woolly.

PEDIGREE VS. REGISTRATION CERTIFICATE

Too often new owners are confused between these two important documents. Your puppy's pedigree, essentially a family tree, is a written record of a dog's genealogy of three generations or more. The pedigree will show you the names as well as performance titles of all dogs in your pup's background. Your breeder must provide you with a registration application, with his part properly filled out. You must complete the application and send it to the AKC with the proper fee.

The seller must provide you with complete records to identify the puppy. The AKC requires that the seller provide the buyer with the following: breed; sex, color and markings; date of birth; litter number (when available); names and registration numbers of the parents; breeder's name; and date sold or delivered.

Color: The colors are silver, apricot-fawn, or black. The silver or apricot-fawn colors should be decided so as to make the contrast complete between the color and the trace and the mask.

Markings: The markings are clearly defined. The muzzle or mask, ears, moles on cheeks, thumb mark or diamond on forehead, and the back trace should be as black as possible. The mask should be black. The more intense and well defined it is, the better. The trace is a black line extending from the occiput to the tail.

Gait: Viewed from the front, the forelegs should be carried well forward, showing no weakness in the pasterns, the paws landing squarely with the central toes straight ahead. The rear action should be strong and free through hocks and stifles, with no twisting or turning in or out at the joints. The hind legs should follow in line with the front. There is a slight natural convergence of the limbs both fore and aft. A slight roll of the hindquarters typifies the gait which should be free, self-assured and jaunty.

Temperament: This is an even-tempered breed, exhibiting stability, playfulness, great charm, dignity and an outgoing, loving disposition.

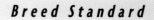

Locating a breeder of quality Pugs and selecting a healthy, friendly, typical Pug puppy are the primary goals of the new Pug owner.

PUG

Before deciding to look for a puppy, it is essential that you are fully clear in your mind that a Pug is the right breed for you and your family. The Pug is a small breed, but is quite a tough little character, in both body and personality. The short coat should not present any problems, but if you have anyone in your family who is prone to allergies, be sure that he will not be affected by a Pug's coat before you make your purchase. Even dogs with short coats shed hair to a certain extent. Regular brushing will limit the amount of hair floating around your home or on your carpets and furniture.

YOUR SCHEDULE . . .

If you lead an erratic, unpredictable life, with daily or weekly changes in your work requirements, consider the problems of owning a puppy. The new puppy has to be fed regularly, socialized (loved, petted, handled, introduced to other people) and, most importantly, allowed to go outdoors for house-training. As the dog gets older, it can be more tolerant of deviations in its feeding and relief schedule.

WHERE TO BEGIN?

If you are convinced that the Pug is the ideal dog for you, it's time to learn about where to find a puppy and what to look for. Locating a litter of Pugs should not present a problem for the new owner. You should inquire about breeders in your area who enjoy a good reputation in the breed. You are looking for an established breeder with outstanding dog ethics and a strong commitment to the breed. New owners should have as many questions as they have doubts. An established breeder is indeed the one to answer your four million questions and make you comfortable with your choice of the Pug. An established breeder will sell you a puppy at a fair price if, and only if, he determines that you are a suitable, worthy owner of his dogs. An established breeder can be relied upon for advice, no matter what time of day or night. A reputable breeder will accept a puppy back, without questions, should you decide that this is not the right dog for you.

When choosing a breeder,

reputation is much more important than convenience of location. Do not be overly impressed by breeders who run brag advertisements in the dog periodicals about their stupendous champions. The real quality breeders are quiet and unassuming. You hear about them at the dog shows and seminars, by word of mouth.

Choosing a breeder is an important first step in dog ownership. Fortunately, the majority of Pug breeders is devoted to the breed and its well-being. New owners should have little problem finding a reputable breeder who doesn't live in a different state or on the other side of the country.

HOW TO SELECT A PUG PUP

Once you have contacted and met a breeder or two and made your choice about which breeder is better suited to your needs, it's time to visit the litter. Keep in mind that many top breeders have waiting lists. Sometimes new owners have to wait as long as two years for a puppy. If you are really committed to the breeder whom you've selected, then you will wait (and hope for an early arrival!). If not, you may have to resort to your second- or third-choice breeder. Don't be too anxious, however. If the breeder doesn't have a waiting

ARE YOU PREPARED?
Unfortunately, when a puppy is bought by someone who does not take into consideration the time and attention that dog ownership requires, it is the puppy who suffers when he is either abandoned or placed in a shelter by a frustrated owner. So all of the "homework" you do in preparation for your pup's arrival will benefit you both. The more informed you are, the more you will know what to expect and the better equipped you will be to handle the ups and downs of raising a puppy. Hopefully, everyone in the household is willing to do his part in raising and caring for the pup. The anticipation of owning a dog often brings a lot of promises from excited family members: "I will walk him every day," "I will feed him," "I will house-train him," etc., but these things require time, effort, consistency, and promises can be easily forgotten once the novelty of the new pet has worn off.

Select a puppy with a lively personality and signs of good health.

must select one from a caring breeder who has given the puppies all the attention they deserve and has looked after them well. A young puppy should look well fed, but not pot-bellied, as this might indicate worms. Take note of the eyes which should look bright and clear, without discharge. Nor, of course, should there be any discharge from the nose and certainly no evidence of loose motions. Always check the bite of your selected puppy to be sure that it is slightly undershot.

The puppy you choose should have a healthy-looking coat and a lively personality. Under no circumstances "take pity on" the weakling of the litter, nor on one that is unduly shy or aggressive.

It is essential that you select a breeder with the utmost care. Initially the American Kennel Club will be able to put you in contact with a breed club, or perhaps directly with breeders, but it is always a good idea to visit a large show at which Pugs will be exhibited. This will provide you with a valuable opportunity to meet various breeders and to see the quality of their stock.

Since you are likely to be choosing a Pug as a pet dog, you simply should select a pup that is friendly and attractive.

list, or any customers, there is probably a good reason. It's no different than visiting a restaurant with no clientele. The better establishments and restaurants always have a waiting list—and it's usually worth the wait. Besides, isn't a puppy more important than a special dinner?

Pug puppies almost invariably look enchanting, but you

ARE YOU A FIT OWNER?

If the breeder from whom you are buying a puppy asks you a lot of personal questions, do not be insulted. Such a breeder wants to be sure that you will be a fit provider for his puppy.

Pugs generally have small litters, averaging four to five puppies (though larger litters are sometimes known), so selection maybe limited once you have located a desirable litter. While the basic structure of the breed has little variation, the temperament may present trouble in certain strains. Beware of the shy or overly aggressive puppy; be especially conscious of the nervous Pug pup. Don't let sentiment or emotion trap you into buying the runt of the litter.

The gender of your puppy is largely a matter of personal taste. Male Pugs show great kindness toward female Pugs and both sexes are extremely placid and "laid back." The difference in size is noticeable but slight. Coloration is not the most important consideration when selecting a Pug. Remember that it will be more difficult to find a good silver pup, as the apricot-fawns are most numerous. The black Pugs, unique in their own right, possess single coats, which may be preferable for the allergic owner.

Breeders commonly allow visitors to see the litter by around the fifth or sixth week, and Pug puppies leave for their new homes around the tenth week. Breeders who permit their puppies to leave early are

TIME TO GO HOME
Breeders rarely release puppies until they are eight to ten weeks of age. This is an acceptable age for most breeds of dog, excepting toy breeds, which are not released until around 10 to 12 weeks, given their petite sizes. If a breeder has a puppy that is 12 weeks of age or older, it is likely well socialized and house-trained. Be sure that it is otherwise healthy before deciding to take it home.

more interested in your money than their puppies' well-being. Puppies need to learn the rules of the pack from their dams, and most dams continue teaching the pups manners and dos and don'ts until around the

TEMPERAMENT COUNTS
Your selection of a good puppy can be determined by your needs. A show potential or a good pet? It is your choice. Every puppy, however, should be of good temperament. Although show-quality puppies are bred and raised with emphasis on physical conformation, responsible breeders strive for equally good temperament. Do not buy from a breeder who concentrates solely on physical beauty at the expense of personality.

eighth week. Breeders spend significant amounts of time with the Pug toddlers so that they are able to interact with the "other species," i.e., humans. Given the long history that dogs and humans have, bonding between the two species is natural but must be nurtured. A well-bred, well-socialized Pug pup wants nothing more than to be near you and please you.

COMMITMENT OF OWNERSHIP
After considering all of these factors, you have most likely already made some very important decisions about selecting your puppy. You have chosen a Pug, which means that you have decided which characteristics you want in a dog and which type of dog will best fit into your family and lifestyle. If you have selected a breeder, you have gone a step further—you have done your research and found a responsible, conscientious person who breeds quality Pugs and who should become a reliable source of help as you and your puppy adjust to life together. If you have observed a litter in action, you have obtained a firsthand look at the dynamics of a puppy "pack" and, thus, you have learned about each pup's individual personality— perhaps you have even found one that particularly appeals to you.

However, even if you have not yet found the Pug puppy of your dreams, observing pups will help you learn to recognize certain behavior and to determine what a pup's behavior indicates about his temperament. You will be able to pick out which pups are the leaders, which ones are less outgoing, which ones are confident, which ones are shy, playful, friendly, aggressive, etc. Equally as important, you will learn to recognize what a healthy pup should look and act like. All of these things will help you in your search, and when you find the Pug that was meant for you, you will know it!

Researching your breed, selecting a responsible breeder and observing as many pups as possible are all important steps on the way to dog ownership. It may seem like a lot of effort… and you have not even taken the pup home yet! Remember, though, you cannot be too careful when it comes to deciding on the type of dog you want and finding out about your prospective pup's background. Buying a puppy is not—or should not be—just another whimsical purchase. This is one instance in which you actually do get to choose your own family! You may be thinking that buying a puppy should be fun—it should not be so serious and so much work. Keep in mind that your puppy is not a cuddly stuffed toy or decorative ornament, but a creature that will become a real

"YOU BETTER SHOP AROUND!"
Finding a reputable breeder that sells healthy pups is very important, but make sure that the breeder you choose is not only someone you respect but also someone with whom you feel comfortable. Your breeder will be a resource long after you buy your puppy, and you must be able to call with reasonable questions without being made to feel like a pest! If you don't connect on a personal level, investigate some other breeders before making a final decision.

member of your family. You will come to realize that, while buying a puppy is a pleasurable and exciting endeavor, it is not something to be taken lightly. Relax...the fun will start when the pup comes home!

Always keep in mind that a puppy is nothing more than a

baby in a furry disguise...a baby who is virtually helpless in a human world and who trusts his owner for fulfillment of his basic needs for survival. In addition to food, water and shelter, your pup needs care, protection, guidance and love. If you are not prepared to commit to this, then you are not prepared to own a dog.

Wait a minute, you say. How hard could this be? All of my neighbors own dogs and they seem to be doing just fine. Why should I have to worry about all of this? Well, you should not worry about it; in fact, you will probably find that once your Pug pup gets used to his new home, he will fall into his place in the family quite naturally. But it never hurts to emphasize the commitment of dog ownership. With some time and patience, it is really not too difficult to raise a curious and exuberant Pug pup to be a well-adjusted and well-mannered adult dog—a dog that could be your most loyal friend.

PREPARING PUPPY'S PLACE IN YOUR HOME

Researching your breed and finding a breeder are only two aspects of the "homework" you will have to do before taking your Pug puppy home. You will also have to prepare your home and family for the new

YOUR PUG PUPPY'S APPEARANCE

Your puppy should have a well-fed appearance but not a distended abdomen, which may indicate worms or incorrect feeding, or both. The body should be firm, with a solid feel. The skin of the abdomen should be pale pink and clean, without signs of scratching or rash. Check the hind legs to make certain that dewclaws were removed by the breeder at birth.

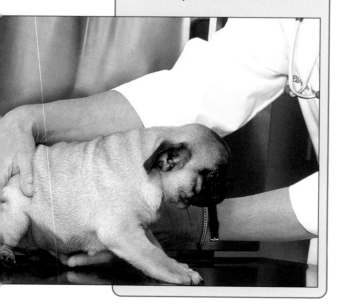

addition. Much as you would prepare a nursery for a newborn baby, you will need to designate a place in your home that will be the puppy's own. How you prepare your home will depend on how much freedom the dog will be allowed. Whatever you decide, you must ensure that he has a place that he can "call his own."

When you bring your new puppy into your home, you are bringing him into what will become his home as well. Obviously, you did not buy a puppy so that he could take control of your house, but in order for a puppy to grow into a stable, well-adjusted dog, he has to feel comfortable in his surroundings. Remember, he is leaving the warmth and security of his mother and littermates, as well as the familiarity of the only place he has ever known, so it is important to make his transition as easy as possible. By preparing a place in your home for the puppy, you are making him feel as welcome as possible in a strange new place. It should not take him long to get used to it, but the sudden shock of being transplanted is somewhat traumatic for a young pup. Imagine how a small child would feel in the same situation—that is how

PUPPY PERSONALITY
When a litter becomes available to you, choosing a pup out of all those adorable faces will not be an easy task! Sound temperament is of utmost importance, but each pup has its own personality and some may be better suited to you than others. A feisty, independent pup will do well in a home with older children and adults, while quiet, shy puppies will thrive in a home with minimal noise and distractions. Your breeder knows the pups best and should be able to guide you in the right direction.

your puppy must be feeling. It is up to you to reassure him and to let him know, "Little fellow, you are going to like it here!"

PHOTO COURTESY OF DOSKOCIL

preferred tool for show puppies as well as pet puppies. Crates are not cruel—crates have many humane and highly effective uses in dog care and training. For example, crate training is a very popular and very successful housebreaking method. A crate can keep your dog safe during travel and, perhaps most importantly, a crate provides your dog with a place of his own in your home. It serves as a "doggie bedroom" of sorts—your Pug can curl up in his crate when he wants to sleep or when he just needs a break. Many dogs sleep in their crates overnight. With soft bedding and his favorite toy, a crate becomes a cozy pseudo-den for your dog. Like his ancestors, he too will seek out

PET INSURANCE

Just like you can insure your car, your house and your own health, you likewise can insure your dog's health. Investigate a pet insurance policy by talking to your vet. Depending on the age of your dog, the breed and the kind of coverage you desire, your policy can be very afford-able. Most policies cover accidental injuries, poisoning and thousands of medical problems and illnesses, including cancers. Some carriers also offer routine care and immunization coverage, including spaying/neutering, health screening and more.

Your local pet shop will have various types of crates suitable for your Pug puppy. Obtain a crate that will be large enough for the full-grown dog.

WHAT YOU SHOULD BUY

CRATE

To someone unfamiliar with the use of crates in dog training, it may seem like punishment to shut a dog in a crate, but this is not the case at all. Most professional dog breeders and trainers are recommending crates as a

the comfort and retreat of a den—you just happen to be providing him with something a little more luxurious than what his early ancestors enjoyed.

As far as purchasing a crate, the type that you buy is up to you. It will most likely be one of the two most popular types: wire or fiberglass. There are advantages and disadvantages to each type. For example, a wire crate is more open, allowing the air to flow through and affording the dog a view of what is going on around him while a fiberglass crate is sturdier. Both can double as travel crates, providing protection for the dog. The size of the crate is another thing to consider. Puppies do not stay puppies forever—in fact, sometimes it seems as if they grow right before your eyes. It is better to get one that will accommodate your dog both as a pup and at full size, even though the Pug doesn't grow too dramatically compared to the larger breeds. A 16" x 18" x 20" crate will be necessary for a full-grown Pug.

BEDDING

A special dog mat in the dog's crate will help the dog feel more at home and you may also like to put in a small blanket. This will take the place of the leaves, twigs, etc., that the pup would use in the wild to make a den; the pup can make his own "burrow" in the crate. Although your pup is far removed from his den-making ancestors, the denning instinct is still a part of his genetic makeup. Second, until you bring your pup home, he has been sleeping amid the warmth of his mother and littermates, and while a blanket is not the same as a warm, breathing body, it still provides heat and something with which to snuggle. You will want to wash your pup's bedding frequently in case he has an accident in his crate, and replace or remove any blanket that becomes ragged and starts to fall apart.

DO YOU WANT TO LIVE LONGER?

If you like to volunteer, it is wonderful if you can take your dog to a nursing home once a week for several hours. The elder community loves to have a dog with which to visit, and often your dog will bring a bit of companionship to someone who is lonely or somewhat detached from the world. You will be not only bringing happiness to someone else but also keeping your dog busy—and we haven't even mentioned the fact that it has been discovered that volunteering helps to increase your own longevity!

CRATE TRAINING TIPS

During crate training, you should partition off the section of the crate in which the pup stays. If he is given too big an area, this will hinder your training efforts. Crate training is based on the fact that a dog does not like to soil his sleeping quarters, so it is ineffective to keep a pup in a crate that is so big that he can eliminate in one end and get far enough away from it to sleep. Also, you want to make the crate den-like for the pup. Blankets and a favorite toy will make the crate cozy for the small pup; as he grows, you may want to evict some of his "roommates" to make more room.

It will take some coaxing at first, but be patient. Given some time to get used to it, your pup will adapt to his new home-within-a-home quite nicely.

Toys

Toys are a must for dogs of all ages, especially for curious playful pups. Puppies are the "children" of the dog world, and what child does not love toys? Chew toys provide enjoyment for both dog and owner—your dog will enjoy playing with his favorite toys, while you will enjoy the fact that they distract him from your expensive shoes and leather sofa. Puppies love to chew; in fact, chewing is a physical need for pups as they are teething, and everything looks appetizing! The full range of your possessions—from dish towel to Oriental carpet—are fair game in the eyes of a teething pup. Puppies are not all that discerning when it comes to finding something to literally "sink their teeth into"—everything tastes great!

Pug puppies are not generally aggressive chewers. Pugs seem to like tennis balls because they are soft and they can easily grip their covering. Toys should not be too hard,

and Pugs should never be allowed to play with sticks, as these can be highly dangerous. Breeders advise owners to resist stuffed toys, because they can become de-stuffed in no time. The overly excited pup may ingest the stuffing, which is neither digestible nor nutritious.

Similarly, squeaky toys are quite popular, but must be avoided for the Pug. Perhaps a squeaky toy can be used as an aid in training, but not for free play. If a pup "disembowels" one of these, the small plastic squeaker inside can be dangerous if swallowed. Monitor the condition of all your pup's toys carefully and get rid of any that have been chewed to the point of becoming potentially dangerous.

Be careful of natural bones, which have a tendency to splinter into sharp, dangerous pieces. Also be careful of rawhide, which can turn into pieces that are easy to swallow and become a mushy mess on your carpet.

LEAD

A nylon lead is probably the best option as it is the most resistant to puppy teeth should your pup take a liking to chewing on his lead. Of course, this is a habit that should be

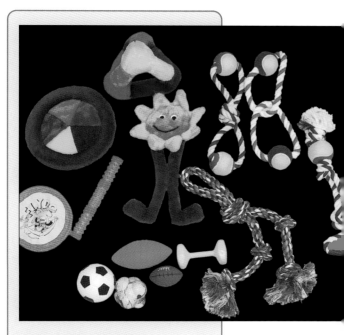

TOYS, TOYS, TOYS!

With a big variety of dog toys available, and so many that look like they would be a lot of fun for a dog, be careful in your selection. It is amazing what a set of puppy teeth can do to an innocent-looking toy; so, obviously, safety is a major consideration. Be sure to choose the most durable products that you can find. Hard nylon bones and toys are a safe bet, and many of them are offered in different scents and flavors that will be sure to capture your dog's attention. It is always fun to play a game of catch with your dog, and there are balls and flying discs that are specially made to withstand dog teeth. Do not offer children's toys to your Pug; use only toys made for dogs.

PLAY'S THE THING

Teaching the puppy to play with his toys in running and fetching games is an ideal way to help the puppy develop muscle, learn motor skills and bond with you, his owner and master. He also needs to learn how to inhibit his bite reflex and never to use his teeth on people, forbidden objects and other animals in play. Puppies traditionally learn the rules of play from their dam and littermates, especially the bite reflex.

Whenever you play with your puppy, you make the rules. This becomes an important message to your puppy in teaching him that you are the pack leader and control everything he does in life. Once your dog accepts you as his leader, your relationship with him will be cemented for life.

Your local pet shop will certainly have many leads from which you can choose one that suits your Pug.

nipped in the bud, but, if your pup likes to chew on his lead, he has a very slim chance of being able to chew through the strong nylon. Nylon leads are also lightweight, which is good for a young Pug who is just getting used to the idea of walking on a lead. For everyday walking and safety purposes, the nylon lead is a good choice. As your pup grows up and gets used to walking on the lead, you may want to purchase a flexible lead. These leads allow you to extend the length to give the dog a broader area to explore or to shorten the length to keep the dog near you. Of course there are special leads for training purposes, and specially made safety harnesses, which might be considered for the Pug who resists a conventional lead or collar.

COLLAR

Your pup should get used to wearing a collar all the time since you will want to attach his ID tags to it. Plus, you have to attach the lead to something! A lightweight nylon collar is a good choice; make sure that it fits snugly enough so that the pup cannot wriggle out of it, but is loose enough so that it will not be uncomfortably tight

MENTAL AND DENTAL

Toys not only help your puppy get the physical and mental stimulation he needs but also provide a great way to keep his teeth clean. Hard rubber or nylon toys, especially those constructed with grooves, are designed to scrape away plaque, preventing bad breath and gum infection and promoting overall dental health.

You may want two sets of bowls, one for inside and one for outside, depending on where the dog will be fed and where he will be spending time. Stainless steel or sturdy plastic bowls are popular choices. Plastic bowls are more chewable. Dogs tend not to chew on the steel variety, which can be sterilized. It is important to buy sturdy bowls since anything is in danger of being chewed by puppy teeth and you do not want your dog to be constantly chewing apart his bowl (for his safety and for your wallet!).

CLEANING SUPPLIES

Until a pup is house-trained, you will be doing a lot of cleaning. "Accidents" will occur, which is acceptable in the beginning because the puppy does not know any

around the pup's neck. You should be able to fit a finger between the pup and the collar. It may take some time for your pup to get used to wearing the collar, but soon he will not even notice that it is there. Choke collars are made for training difficult dogs, but should not be used on the Pug.

FOOD AND WATER BOWLS

Your pup will need two bowls, one for food and one for water.

If you are seeking a Pug puppy for showing, discuss this with your breeder. Future show stars need to be trained for the ring at an early age.

Your local pet shop sells an array of dishes and bowls for water and food. Consider elevating your Pug's bowl as a preventative measure against bloat.

PHOTO COURTESY OF MIDKI PET PRODUCTS.

better. All you can do is be prepared to clean up any accidents. Old rags, towels, newspapers and a safe disinfectant are good to have on hand.

BEYOND THE BASICS
The items previously discussed are the bare necessities. You will find out what else you need as you go along—grooming supplies, flea/tick protection, baby gates to partition a room, etc. These things will vary depending on your situation, but it is important that you have everything you need to feed and make your Pug comfortable in his first few days at home.

PUPPY-PROOFING YOUR HOME
Aside from making sure that your Pug will be comfortable in your home, you also have to make sure that your home is safe for your Pug. This means taking precautions that your pup will not get into anything he should not get into and that there is nothing within his reach that may harm him should he sniff it, chew it, inspect it, etc. This probably seems obvious since, while you are primarily concerned with your pup's safety, at the same time you do not want your belongings to be ruined. Breakables should be placed

CHOOSE AN APPROPRIATE COLLAR

The **BUCKLE COLLAR** is the standard collar used for everyday purpose. Be sure that you adjust the buckle on growing puppies. Check it every day. It can become too tight overnight! These collars can be made of leather or nylon. Attach your dog's identification tags to this collar.

The **CHOKE COLLAR** is constructed of highly polished steel so that it slides easily through the stainless steel loop. The idea is that the dog controls the pressure around his neck and he will stop pulling if the collar becomes uncomfortable. This collar is not appropriate for the Pug.

The **HARNESS or HALTER** is for a trained dog that has to be restrained to prevent running away, chasing a cat and the like. Considered the most humane of all collars, it is frequently used on smaller dogs for which collars are not comfortable.

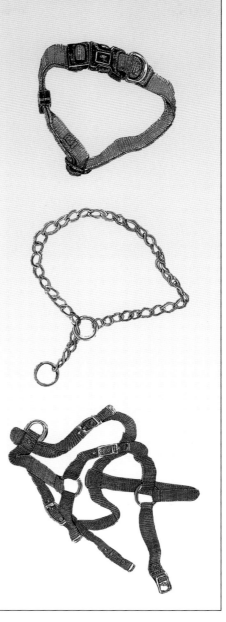

chemicals where the pup cannot reach them.

It is also important to make sure that the outside of your home is safe. Of course, your puppy should never be unsupervised, but a pup let loose in the yard will want to run and explore, and he should be granted that freedom. Do not let a fence give you a false sense of security. Although most Pugs are not "escape artists," you would be surprised how crafty (and persistent) a dog can be in figuring out how to dig under and squeeze his way through small holes, or to climb over a fence. The remedy is to make the fence well embedded into the ground and high enough so that it really is impossible for your dog to get over it (about 5 feet should suffice). Be sure to repair or secure any gaps in the

out of reach if your dog is to have full run of the house. If he is to be limited to certain places within the house, keep any potentially dangerous items in the "off-limits" areas. An electrical cord can pose a danger should the puppy decide to taste it—and who is going to convince a pup that it would not make a great chew toy? Cords should be fastened tightly against the wall. If your dog is going to spend time in a crate, make sure that there is nothing near his crate that he can reach if he sticks his curious little nose or paws through the openings. Just as you would with a child, keep all household cleaners and

PUPPY FEEDING

You will probably start feeding your pup the same food that he has been getting from the breeder; the breeder should give you a few days' supply to start you off. Although you should not give your pup too many treats, you will want to have puppy treats on hand for training. Be careful, though, as a small pup's calorie requirements are relatively low and a few treats can add up to almost a full day's worth of calories without the required nutrition.

fence and check the fence periodically to ensure that it is still sound. A very determined pup may return to the same spot to "work on it" until he is able to get through.

FIRST TRIP TO THE VET

You have selected your puppy, and your home and family are ready. Now all you have to do is collect your Pug from the breeder and the fun begins,

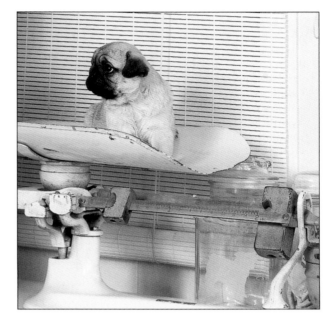

> ### SKULL & CROSSBONES
> Thoroughly puppy-proof your house before bringing your puppy home. Never use cockroach or rodent poisons or plant fertilizers in any area accessible to the puppy. Avoid the use of toilet cleaners. Most dogs are born with "toilet-bowl sonar" and will take a drink if the lid is left open. Also keep the trash secured and out of reach.

right? Well…not so fast. Something else you need to prepare is your pup's first trip to the veterinarian. Perhaps the breeder can recommend someone in the area who specializes in Pugs, or maybe you know some other Pug owners who can suggest a good vet. Either way, you should have an appointment arranged for your pup before you pick him up.

The pup's first visit will consist of an overall examination to make sure that the pup does not have any problems that are not apparent to you. The veterinarian will also set up a schedule for the pup's vaccinations; the breeder

One of the most important considerations when evaluating the health of a new puppy is its weight. The veterinarian will weigh the puppy and then monitor its development over the next few months.

NATURAL TOXINS

Examine your lawn and home landscaping before bringing your puppy home. Many varieties of plants have leaves, stems or flowers that are toxic if ingested, and you can depend on a curious puppy to investigate them. Ask your vet for information on poisonous plants or research them at your library.

should inform you of which ones the pup has already received and the vet can continue from there.

INTRODUCTION TO THE FAMILY

Everyone in the house will be excited about the puppy's coming home and will want to pet him and play with him, but it is best to make the introduction low-key so as not to overwhelm the puppy. He is apprehensive already. It is the first time he has been separated from his mother and the breeder, and the ride to your home is likely to be the first time he has been in a car. The last thing you want to do is smother him, as this will only frighten him further. This is not to say that human contact is not extremely necessary at this stage, because this is the time when a connection between the pup and his human family is formed. Gentle petting and soothing words should help console him, as well as just putting him down and letting him explore on his own (under your watchful eye, of course).

The pup may approach the family members or may busy himself with exploring for a while. Gradually, each person should spend some time with the pup, one at a time, crouching down to get as close to the pup's level as possible and letting him sniff their hands and petting him gently. He definitely needs human attention and he needs to be touched—this is how to form an immediate bond. Just remember that the pup is experiencing a lot of things for the first time, at the same time. There are new people, new noises, new smells and new things to investigate, so be gentle, be affectionate and be as comforting as you can be.

PUP'S FIRST NIGHT HOME

You have traveled home with your new charge safely in his crate. He's been to the vet for a thorough check-up; he's been weighed, his papers examined; perhaps he's even been vaccinated and wormed as well. He's met the family and he's licked the whole family, including the excited children and the less-than-happy cat. He's explored his area, his new bed, the yard and anywhere else he's been permitted. He's eaten his first meal at home and relieved himself in the proper place. He's heard lots of new sounds, smelled new friends and seen more of the outside world than ever before. That was just the first day! He's worn out and is ready for bed...or so you think!

It's puppy's first night and

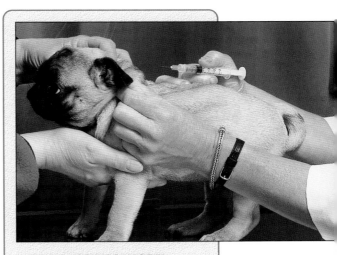

HOW VACCINES WORK

If you've just bought a puppy, you surely know the importance of having your pup vaccinated, but do you understand how vaccines work? Vaccines contain the same bacteria or viruses that cause the disease you want to prevent, but they have been chemically modified so that they don't cause any harm. Instead, the vaccine causes your dog to produce antibodies that fight the harmful bacteria. Thus, if your pup is exposed to the disease in the future, the antibodies will destroy the viruses or bacteria.

you are ready to say "Good night"—keep in mind that this is puppy's first night ever to be sleeping alone. His dam and littermates are no longer at paw's length and he's a bit scared, cold and lonely. Be reassuring to your new family

Children are a part of every pup's socialization process. Keep an eye on an encounters with young people and small puppies. Pugs are solid but delicate little dogs and can be injured if carelessly handled.

member. This is not the time to spoil him and give in to his inevitable whining.

Puppies whine. They whine to let others know where they are and hopefully to get company out of it. Place your pup in his new bed or crate in his room and close the door. Mercifully, he may fall asleep without a peep. If the inevitable occurs, ignore the whining: he is fine. Be strong and keep his interest in mind. Do not allow yourself to feel guilty and visit the pup. He will fall asleep eventually.

Many breeders recommend placing a piece of bedding from his former home in his new bed so that the pup recognizes the scent of his littermates. Others still advise placing a hot water bottle in his bed for warmth. This latter may be a good idea

provided the pup doesn't attempt to suckle—he'll get good and wet and may not fall asleep so fast.

Puppy's first night can be somewhat stressful for the pup and his new family. Remember that you are setting the tone of nighttime at your house. Unless you want to play with your pup every evening at 10 p.m., midnight and 2 a.m., don't initiate the habit. Your family will thank you, and so will your pup!

THE COCOA WARS

Chocolate contains the chemical thebromine, which is poisonous to dogs, although "chocolates" especially made for dogs are safe (as they don't actually contain thebromine) but not recommended. Any item that encourages your dog to enjoy the taste of cocoa should be discouraged. You should also exercise caution when using mulch in your garden. This frequently contains cocoa hulls, and dogs have been known to die from eating mulch.

PREVENTING PUPPY PROBLEMS

SOCIALIZATION

Now that you have done all of the preparatory work and have helped your pup get accustomed to his new home and family, it is about time for you to have some fun! Socializing your Pug pup gives you the opportunity to show off your new friend, and your pup gets to reap the benefits of being an adorable furry creature that people will want to pet and, in general, think is absolutely precious!

Besides getting to know his new family, your puppy should be exposed to other people, animals and situations. This will help him become well adjusted as he grows up and less prone to being timid or fearful of the new things he will encounter. Of course, he must not come into close contact with dogs you don't know well until his course of injections is fully complete. Your pup's socialization began with the breeder, but now it is your responsibility to continue it. The socialization he receives up until the age of 12 weeks is the most critical, as this is the time when he forms his impressions of the outside world. Be especially careful during the eight-to-ten-week-old period,

also known as the fear period. The interaction he receives during this time should be gentle and reassuring. Lack of socialization can manifest itself in fear and aggression as the

> **STRESS-FREE**
> Some experts in canine health advise that stress during a dog's early years of development can compromise and weaken his immune system, and may trigger the potential for a shortened life. They emphasize the need for happy and stress-free growing-up years.

Your family takes over where your puppy's siblings left off. You become the pup's family and he relies upon you for security, love and proper care.

dog grows up. He needs lots of human contact, affection, handling and exposure to other animals.

Once your pup has received his necessary vaccinations, feel free to take him out and about (on his lead, of course). Walk him around the neighborhood, take him on your daily errands, let people pet him, let him meet other dogs and pets, etc. Puppies do not have to try to make friends; there will be no shortage of people who will want to introduce themselves. Just make sure that you carefully supervise each meeting. If the neighborhood children want to say hello, for example, that is great—children and pups most often make great companions. Sometimes an excited child can unintention-

ally handle a pup too roughly, or an overzealous pup can playfully nip a little too hard. You want to make socialization experiences positive ones. What a pup learns during this very formative stage will affect his attitude toward future encounters. You want your dog to be comfortable around

SOCIALIZATION

Thorough socialization includes not only meeting new people but also being introduced to new experiences such as riding in the car, having his coat brushed, hearing the television, walking in a crowd—the list is endless. The more your pup experiences, and the more positive the experiences are, the less of a shock and the less frightening it will be for your pup to encounter new things.

everyone. A pup that has a bad experience with a child may grow up to be a dog that is shy around or aggressive toward children.

CONSISTENCY IN TRAINING

Dogs, being pack animals, naturally need a leader, or else they try to establish dominance in their packs. When you welcome a dog into your family, the choice of who becomes the leader and who becomes the "pack" is entirely up to you! Your pup's intuitive quest for dominance, coupled with the fact that it is nearly impossible to look at an adorable Pug pup with his "puppy-dog" eyes and not cave in, give the pup almost an unfair advantage in getting the upper hand! A pup will definitely test the waters to see what he can and cannot do. Do not give in to those pleading eyes—stand your ground when it comes to disciplining the pup and make sure that all family members do the same. It will only confuse the pup when Mother tells him to get off the couch when he is used to sitting up there with Father to watch the nightly news. Avoid discrepancies by having all members of the household decide on the rules before the pup even comes home...and be consistent in enforcing them!

MANNERS MATTER

During the socialization process, a puppy should meet people, experience different environments and definitely be exposed to other canines. Through playing and interacting with other dogs, your puppy will learn lessons, ranging from controlling the pressure of his jaws by biting his littermates to the inner-workings of the canine pack that he will apply to his human relationships for the rest of his life. That is why removing a puppy from its litter too early can be detrimental to the pup's development. Some small breeds are not removed until ten weeks of age or older.

PROPER SOCIALIZATION
The socialization period for puppies is from age 8 to 16 weeks. This is the time when puppies need to leave their birth family and take up residence with their new owners, where they will meet many new people, other pets, etc. Failure to be adequately socialized can cause the dog to grow up fearing others and being shy and unfriendly due to a lack of self-confidence.

Early training shapes the dog's personality, so you cannot be unclear in what you expect.

COMMON PUPPY PROBLEMS
The best way to prevent puppy problems is to be proactive in stopping an undesirable behavior as soon as it starts. The old saying "You can't teach an old dog new tricks" does not necessarily hold true, but it is true that it is much easier to discourage bad behavior in a young developing pup than to wait until the pup's bad behavior becomes the adult dog's bad habit. There are some problems that are especially prevalent in puppies as they develop.

NIPPING
As puppies start to teethe, they feel the need to sink their teeth into anything available... unfortunately that includes your fingers, arms, hair and toes. You may find this behavior cute for the first five seconds... until you feel just how sharp those puppy teeth are. This is something you want to discourage immediately and consistently with a firm "No!" (or whatever number of firm "Nos" it takes for him to understand that you mean business). Then replace your finger with an appropriate chew toy. While this behavior is merely annoying when the dog is young, it can become dangerous as your Pug's adult teeth grow in and his jaws develop, and he continues to think it is okay to gnaw on human appendages. Your Pug

does not mean any harm with a friendly nip, but he also does not know his own strength.

CRYING/WHINING

Your pup will often cry, whine, whimper, howl or make some type of commotion when he is left alone. This is basically his way of calling out for attention to make sure that you know he is there and that you have not forgotten about him. He feels insecure when he is left alone,

CHEWING TIPS

Chewing goes hand in hand with nipping in the sense that a teething puppy is always looking for a way to soothe his aching gums. In this case, instead of chewing on you, he may have taken a liking to your favorite shoe or something else which he should not be chewing. Again, realize that this is a normal canine behavior that does not need to be discouraged, only redirected. Your pup just needs to be taught what is acceptable to chew on and what is off-limits. Consistently tell him NO when you catch him chewing on something forbidden and give him a chew toy.

Conversely, praise him when you catch him chewing on something appropriate. In this way you are discouraging the inappropriate behavior and reinforcing the desired behavior. The puppy's chewing should stop after his adult teeth have come in, but an adult dog continues to chew for various reasons—perhaps because he is bored, needs to relieve tension or just likes to chew. That is why it is important to redirect his chewing when he is still young.

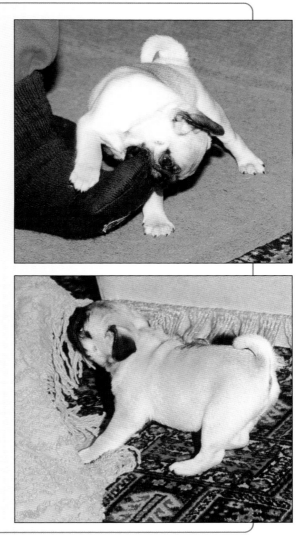

By and large, Pugs are house dogs who are most comfortable indoors. Your Pug puppy will take a few days to start feeling at home, but, when he does, he'll gladly assume a soft, cozy throne.

when you are out of the house and he is in his crate or when you are in another part of the house and he cannot see you. The noise he is making is an expression of the anxiety he feels at being alone, so he needs to be taught that being alone is okay. You are not actually training the dog to stop making noise, you are training him to feel comfortable when he is alone and thus removing the need for him to make the noise.

This is where the crate with cozy bedding and a toy comes in handy. You want to know that he is safe when you are not there to supervise, and you know that he will be safe in his crate rather than roaming freely about the house. In order for the pup to stay in his crate without making a fuss, he needs to be comfortable in his crate. On that note, it is extremely important that the crate is never used as a form of punishment, or the pup will have a negative association with the crate.

Accustom the pup to the crate in short, gradually increasing time intervals in which you put him in the crate, maybe with a treat, and stay in the room with him. If he cries or makes a fuss, do not go to him, but stay in his sight. Gradually he will realize that staying in his crate is all right without your help, and it will

not be so traumatic for him when you are not around. You may want to leave the radio on softly when you leave the house; the sound of human voices may be comforting to him.

PUPPY PROBLEMS
The majority of problems that are commonly seen in young pups will disappear as your dog gets older. However, how you deal with problems when he is young will determine how he reacts to discipline as an adult dog. It is important to establish who is boss (hopefully it will be you!) right away when you are first bonding with your dog. This bond will set the tone for the rest of your life together.

FOOD PREFERENCE

Selecting the best dry dog food is difficult. There is no majority consensus among veterinary scientists as to the value of nutrient analysis (protein, fat, fiber, moisture, ash, cholesterol, minerals, etc.). All agree that feeding trials are what matter, but you also have to consider the individual dog. The dog's weight, age and activity level, and what pleases his taste, all must be considered. It is probably best to take the advice of your veterinarian. Every dog's dietary requirements vary, even during the lifetime of a particular dog.

If your dog is fed a good dry food, it does not require supplements of meat or vegetables. Dogs do appreciate a little variety in their diets, so you may choose to stay with the same brand but vary the flavor. Alternatively, you may wish to add a little flavored stock to give a difference to the taste.

DIETARY AND FEEDING CONSIDERATIONS

Pugs can undoubtedly be greedy eaters, so it is important not to allow your dog to overeat. A Pug that is overweight has additional strain put on both the heart and on the joints, and any overweight dog is at greater risk under anesthesia. Also, old Pugs that are carrying too much weight can have great difficulty in using their back legs well, another reason why sensible dietary control is important.

Some Pug owners like to feed just one meal each day, perhaps with a small snack at the other end of the day; others prefer to feed two smaller meals each day. There are now numerous high-quality canine meals available and one of them will certainly suit your own Pug. When you bought your puppy, the breeder should have provided you with a diet sheet giving details of exactly how your puppy has been fed. Of course, you are at liberty to change that food, and will need to do so as the youngster reaches adulthood, but this should be done gradually. If you have chosen your breeder well, you should be able to obtain sound

advice about which food is considered most suitable for his line of Pugs.

Many Pug owners like to add a little cooked chicken to dry foods, though one must always bear in mind that, in adding items to complete diets, one is technically "unbalancing" that diet. Some Pug breeders and owners still cook for their dogs every day, preferring to give fresh food.

Today the choices of food for your Pug are many and varied. There are simply dozens of brands of food in all sorts of flavors and textures, ranging from puppy diets to those for seniors. There are even hypoallergenic and low-calorie diets available. Because your Pug's food has a bearing on coat, health and temperament, it is essential that the most suitable diet is selected for a Pug of his age. It is fair to say, however, that even experienced owners can be perplexed by the enormous range of foods available. Only understanding what is best for your dog will help you reach an informed decision.

Dog foods are produced in three basic types: dry, semi-moist and canned. Dry foods are useful for the cost-conscious for overall they tend to be less expensive than semi-moist or canned. They also contain the least fat and the most preservatives. In general, canned foods are made up of 60–70% water, while semi-moist ones often contain so much sugar that they are perhaps the least preferred by owners, even though

The puppy will be weaned from its mother and eating solid food before the new owner assumes responsibility for the Pug. Discuss feeding plans with your breeder.

their dogs seem to like them.

When selecting your dog's diet, three stages of development must be considered: the puppy stage, adult stage and the senior stage.

PUPPY STAGE

Puppies instinctively want to suck milk from their mother's teats and a normal puppy will exhibit this behavior from just a few moments following birth. If puppies do not attempt to suckle within the first half-hour or so, they should be encouraged to do so by placing them on the nipples, having selected ones with plenty of milk. This early milk supply is important in providing colostrum to protect the puppies during the first eight to ten weeks of their lives. Although a mother's milk is much better than any milk formula, despite there being some

Pregnant and lactating bitches will require different dietary needs than other dogs. After the puppies have been weaned, the bitch can resume her normal diet.

> ### GRAIN-BASED DIETS
> Some less expensive dog foods are based on grains and other plant proteins. While these products may appear to be attractively priced, many breeders prefer a diet based on animal proteins and believe that they are more conducive to your dog's health. Many grain-based diets rely on soy protein, which may cause flatulence (passing gas).
>
> There are many cases, however, when your dog might require a special diet. These special requirements should only be recommended by your veterinarian.

excellent ones available, if the puppies do not feed, the breeder will have to feed them himself. For those with less experience, advice from a veterinarian is important so that not only the right quantity of milk is fed but also that of correct quality, fed at suitably frequent intervals, usually every two hours during the first few days of life.

Puppies should be allowed to nurse from their mothers for about the first six weeks, although from the third or fourth week the breeder will begin to introduce small portions of suitable solid food. Most breeders like to introduce alternate milk and meat meals initially, building up to weaning time.

By the time the puppies are

CORRECT BODY WEIGHT

While humans may obsess about how they look and how trim their bodies are, many people believe that extra weight on their dogs is a good thing. The truth is, pets should not be over- or under-weight, as both can lead to or signal sickness. In order to tell how fit your pet is, run your hands over his ribs. Are his ribs buried under a layer of fat or are they sticking out considerably? If your pet is within his normal weight range, you should be able to feel the ribs easily, but they should not protrude abnormally. If you stand above him, the outline of his body should resemble an hourglass. Some breeds do tend to be leaner while some are a bit stockier, but making sure your dog is the right weight for his breed will certainly contribute to his good health.

seven or a maximum of eight weeks old, they should be fully weaned and fed solely on a propri-etary puppy food. Selection of the most suitable, good-quality diet at this time is essential, for a puppy's fastest growth rate is during the first year of life. Veterinarians are usually able to offer advice in this regard. The frequency of meals will be reduced over time, and Pugs are kept on a puppy diet until at least 12 months of age.

ADULT DIETS

Some breeders and exhibitors keep their Pugs on puppy food all their lives. Other people move onto a junior food at about 12 months. However, few Pug dog owners feed ready-prepared adult food because the pieces of most brands are too large. Some companies offer a small-bite variety.

Quality dog food should be well balanced for the needs of your dog, so that except in certain circumstances additional vitamins, minerals and proteins will not be required.

TIPPING THE SCALES

Good nutrition is vital to your dog's health, but many people end up over-feeding or giving unnecessary supplements. Here are some common doggie diet don'ts:

• Adding milk, yogurt and cheese to your dog's diet may seem like a good idea for coat and skin care, but dairy products are very fattening and can cause indigestion.
• Diets high in fat will not cause heart attacks in dogs but will certainly cause your dog to gain weight.
• Most importantly, don't assume your Pug will simply stop eating once he doesn't need any more food. Given the chance, he will eat you out of house and home!

SENIOR DIETS

As dogs get older, their metabolism changes. The older dog usually exercises less, moves more slowly and sleeps more. This change in lifestyle and physiological performance requires a change in diet in some breeds, although many Pug owners never change to a senior diet.

As your dog gets older, few of his organs function up to par. The kidneys slow down and the intestines become less efficient. These age-related factors are sometimes handled with a change in diet or feeding schedule to give smaller portions that are more easily digested.

There is no single best diet for every older dog. While many dogs do well on light or senior diets, other dogs do better on puppy diets or other special premium diets such as lamb and rice. Be sensitive to your senior Pug's diet and this will help control other problems that may arise with your old friend.

WATER

Just as your dog needs proper nutrition from his food, water is an essential "nutrient" as well. Water keeps the dog's body properly hydrated and promotes normal function of the body's systems. During housebreaking, it is necessary to keep an eye on how much water your Pug is drinking, but once he is reliably trained he

A Worthy Investment

Veterinary studies have proven that a balanced high-quality diet pays off in your dog's coat quality, behavior and activity level. Invest in premium brands for the maximum payoff with your dog.

DRINK, DRANK, DRUNK— MAKE IT A DOUBLE

In both humans and dogs, as well as most other living organisms, water forms the major part of nearly every body tissue. Naturally, we take water for granted, but without it, life as we know it would cease.

For dogs, water is needed to keep their bodies functioning biochemically. Additionally, water is needed to replace the water lost while panting. Unlike humans, who are able to sweat to dissipate heat, dogs must pant to cool down, thereby losing the vital water from their bodies needed to regulate their body temperatures. Humans lose electrolyte-containing products and other body-fluid components through sweating; dogs do not lose anything except water.

Water is essential always, but especially so when the weather is hot or humid or when your dog is exercising or playing vigorously.

should have access to clean fresh water at all times, especially if you feed dry food. Make certain that the dog's water bowl is clean, and change the water often.

EXERCISE

The Pug should be a sturdy and muscular little dog, and he needs more exercise than you might expect. Having said that, the Pug seems ready to accept as much or as little exercise as his owner will give him. Muscles need to be kept in good, firm condition, so adequate exercise is a must. However, Pugs should always have access to water and it is wise to carry a small container of water on any walk.

Because the Pug is small, it is not necessary to take your Pug on long walks, nor is vigorous exercise essential. Important, though, is walking your Pug on a lead at a steady pace a couple of times each day. Walking not only on soft, grassy surfaces but also on firm ones will help to maintain muscle tone, tighten the feet and keep nail cutting to a minimum. Pugs like the sun but should never be exercised in hot weather. Black Pugs are particularly affected by the heat. In the summer, it is wisest to walk your Pug in the early morning or evening, when it is cooler. Should your Pug get wet while walking, he should be dried down thoroughly upon his return home as long-term exposure to dampness can result in aching limbs for the older dog.

All dogs require some form of exercise, regardless of breed. A sedentary lifestyle is as harmful to a dog as it is to a person. Bear in mind that an overweight dog should never be suddenly over-exercised; instead, he should be encouraged to increase exercise slowly. Not only is exercise essential to keep the dog's body fit, it is essential to his mental well-being. A bored dog will find something to do, which often manifests itself in some type of destructive behavior. In this sense, exercise is essential for the owner's mental well-being as well!

GROOMING
Although the Pug has a short coat that is much less demanding than the coats of many other breeds, coat care should never be overlooked. Ideally you should check over your dog's coat at least every couple of days, also paying close attention to eyes, ears, wrinkles and feet.

HEAD, EYES AND EARS
The wrinkles over the nose must never be allowed to get sore, so at the very first sign that something is not as it should be, the area should be carefully wiped clean and smeared with pure lanolin or petroleum jelly. Some owners

FEEDING TIPS
Dog food must be at room temperature, neither too hot nor too cold. Fresh water, changed often and served in a clean bowl, is mandatory, especially when feeding dry food.

Never feed your dog from the table while you are eating, and never feed your dog leftovers from your own meal. They usually contain too much fat and too much seasoning, plus feeding from the table can initiate other bad habits.

Dogs must chew their food. Hard pellets are excellent; soups and stews are to be avoided. Don't add any extras to normal dog food without first consulting your vet. The normal food is usually balanced, and adding something extra destroys the balance.

Except for age-related changes, dogs do not require dietary variations. They can be fed the same diet, day after day, without becoming ill.

Your local pet shop will have all the grooming tools necessary to keep your Pug's coat in perfect condition. Short-haired dogs like Pugs are easier to maintain than longer-coated breeds.

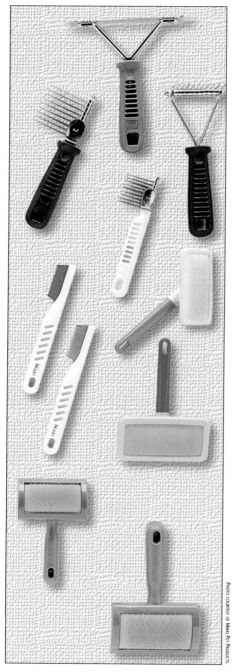

PHOTO COURTESY OF MIKKI PET PRODUCTS.

prefer to use Hibiscrub, an antimicrobial preparation used for pre-surgery hand disinfection; this also helps clear any infection. Black Pugs are rather prone to having their wrinkles become over-greasy, so this will also need to be checked. While considering this aspect of the Pug's face, it is also important never to let the nose itself become too dry, as this can sometimes happen in the breed.

Eyes and ears should also be carefully wiped clean. If necessary, use one of the proprietary cleansers available from good pet shops and other canine outlets. Make sure that a separate cotton ball or tissue is used for each eye and ear, so that there is no transfer of infection. Always check especially for any build-up

GROOMING EQUIPMENT

How much grooming equipment you purchase will depend on how much grooming you are going to do.
• Natural-bristle brush
• Slicker brush
• Metal comb
• Hound-glove
• Scissors
• Blow dryer
• Rubber mat
• Dog shampoo
• Spray hose attachment
• Ear cleaner
• Cotton balls
• Towels
• Nail clippers or file

of wax in the ear. This seems to occur with greater frequency in black Pugs. If caught early enough, a waxy build-up within the ear should be easy enough to cleanse, but never probe into the ear, as doing so can cause injury within the canal.

Be on the lookout for any signs of infection or ear-mite infestation. If your Pug has been shaking his head or scratching at his ears, this usually indicates a problem. If his ears have an unusual odor, this is a sure sign of mite infestation or infection, and a signal to have his ears checked by the veterinarian.

When grooming your Pug, don't neglect his eyes. Cleaning the eyes with a cotton ball will keep debris from building up and causing irritation.

A regular once-over on your Pug's coat with a grooming glove will keep him looking his best.

A grooming rake is an effective way to remove dead hair and undercoat from the apricot-fawn or silver Pug's double coat.

FEET

When inspecting feet, you must check not only the nails but also the pads of the feet. Take care that the pads have not become cracked and always check between the pads to be sure that nothing has become lodged there. Depending upon the season, there may be a danger of grass seeds or thorns becoming embedded, or even tar from the road getting stuck. Butter, by the way, is useful to help remove tar from his feet.

NAIL CLIPPING

Your Pug should be accustomed to having his nails trimmed at an early age, since it will be part of your maintenance routine throughout his life. Not only does it look nicer, but long nails can scratch someone unintentionally. Also, a long nail has a better chance of ripping and bleeding, or causing the feet to spread. A good rule of thumb is that if you can hear your dog's nails' clicking on the floor when he walks, his nails are too long. How frequently nails need to be clipped will depend very much on how often your Pug walks on hard surfaces.

Before you start cutting, make sure you can identify the "quick" in each nail. This can be difficult in the Pug because most Pugs have black nails. The quick is a blood vessel that runs through the center of each nail and grows rather close to the end. It will bleed if accidentally cut, which will be quite painful for the dog as it contains nerve endings. If ever bleeding does accidentally occur, this can be easily stemmed by using potassium permanganate. This is available from your vet, so it is always worth keeping a small supply in your medicine cabinet, but, in an emergency, household flour or a styptic pencil or styptic powder (the type used for shaving) will have similar effect and stop the bleeding quickly when applied to the end of the cut nail. Do not panic if you cut the quick, just stop the bleeding and talk soothingly to your dog. Once he has calmed down, move on to the next nail. Always clip a little at a time, as black nails are more difficult to trim because you can not see the quick.

Hold your pup steady as you begin trimming his nails; you do not want him to make any sudden movements or run away. Talk to him soothingly and stroke

PEDICURE TIP

A dog that spends a lot of time outside on a hard surface, such as cement or pavement, will have his nails naturally worn down and may not need to have them trimmed as often, except maybe in the colder months when he is not outside as much. Regardless, it is best to get your dog accustomed to the nail-trimming procedure at an early age so that he is used to it. Some dogs are especially sensitive about having their feet touched, but if a dog has experienced it since puppyhood, it should not bother him.

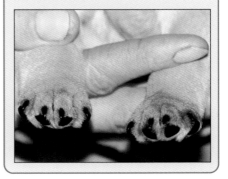

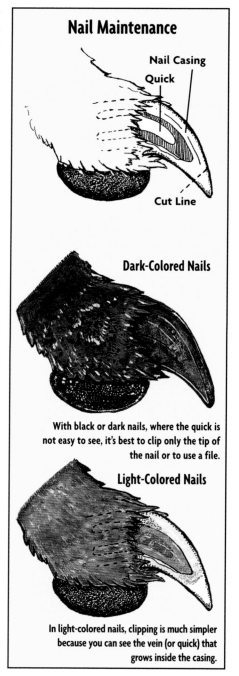

Nail Maintenance

Nail Casing

Quick

Cut Line

Dark-Colored Nails

With black or dark nails, where the quick is
not easy to see, it's best to clip only the tip of
the nail or to use a file.

Light-Colored Nails

In light-colored nails, clipping is much simpler
because you can see the vein (or quick) that
grows inside the casing.

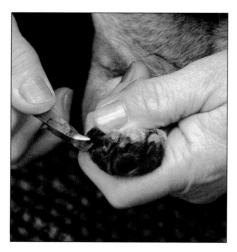

him as you clip. Holding his foot in your hand, simply take off the end of each nail in one quick clip. You can purchase nail clippers that are specially made for dogs; you can probably find them wherever you buy pet or grooming supplies.

TEETH

Teeth should always be kept as free from tartar as possible, but many Pugs do not take kindly to having their teeth cleaned either with a tooth-scraper or with canine toothpaste, as is more usual for most other breeds. Allowing your Pug to chew on a nylon bone or small, hard biscuits will certainly help in this regard, but Pugs do tend to lose their teeth at an early age.

It is possible to get one's vet to check teeth under anesthesia, but some experienced owners do not like their Pugs to be given anesthetics when they are over six years of age; discuss anesthesia sensitivity with the vet.

COAT

When grooming the coat, some owners like to initially comb through with a fine-toothed steel comb. This serves to remove any loose hair and should provide a good indicator of whether there is any build-up of dirt in the coat, necessitating a bath. However, other owners, especially those who groom their dogs regularly for shows, find that they manage fine without a comb at all, using a brush instead.

Even if you have combed thoroughly, a soft bristle brush should be used to go through the coat again. Then use a hound-glove that serves the dual purpose of grooming the coat and massaging the skin. Finally, go over the coat either with chamois leather or a piece of velvet, just to put the final touch, leaving a good sheen on the coat.

Many owners of show Pugs like to bathe their dogs before each show, and this is almost certainly necessary for blacks.

BATHING

Dogs do not need to be bathed as often as humans, but regular bathing is essential for healthy skin and a healthy, shiny coat. Again, like most anything, if you accustom your pup to being bathed as a puppy, it will be second nature by the time he grows up. You want your dog to be at ease in the bathtub or else it could end up a wet, soapy, messy ordeal for both of you!

Brush your Pug thoroughly

LET THE SUN SHINE

Your dog needs daily sunshine for the same reason people do. Pets kept inside homes with curtains drawn against the sun suffer from "SAD" (Seasonal Affected Disorder) to the same degree as humans. We now know that sunlight must enter the iris and thus progress to the pineal gland to regulate the body's hormonal system. When we live and work in artificial light, both circadian rhythms and hormone balances are disturbed.

before wetting his coat. Make certain that your dog has a good non-slip surface to stand on. Begin by wetting the dog's coat. A shower or hose attachment is necessary for thoroughly wetting and rinsing the coat. Check the water temperature to make sure that it is neither too hot nor too cold.

Next, apply shampoo to the dog's coat and work it into a good lather. You should purchase a shampoo that is made for dogs. Do not use a product made for human hair. Wash the head last; you do not want shampoo to drip into the dog's eyes while you are washing the rest of his body. Work the shampoo all the way down to the skin. You can use this opportunity to check the skin for any bumps, bites or other abnormalities. Do not neglect any area of the body— get all of the hard-to-reach places.

Once the dog has been thoroughly shampooed, he requires an equally thorough rinsing. Shampoo left in the coat can be irritating to the skin. Protect his eyes from the shampoo by shielding them with your hand and directing the flow of water in the opposite direction. You should also avoid getting water in the ear canal. Be prepared for your dog to shake out his coat— you might want to stand back, but make sure you have a hold on the dog to keep him from running through the house.

Begin training Pug puppies to accept brushing so that they are amenable to grooming as adults.

SOAP IT UP

The use of human soap products like shampoo, bubble bath and hand soap can be damaging to a dog's coat and skin. Human products are too strong; they remove the protective oils coating the dog's hair and skin that make him water-resistant. Use only shampoo made especially for dogs, which you can find at your local pet shop. You may like to use a medicated shampoo, which will help to keep external parasites at bay.

An ex-pen is an ideal addition to your traveling equipment. These portable wire enclosures give your Pug off-lead time to stretch his legs, eat and play while in a strange area.

TRAVELING WITH YOUR DOG

CAR TRAVEL

You should accustom your Pug to riding in a car at an early age. You may or may not take him in the car often, but at the very least he will need to go to the vet and you do not want these trips to be traumatic for the dog or troublesome for you. The safest way for a dog to ride in the car is in his crate. If he uses a crate in the house, you can use the same crate for travel.

Put the pup in the crate and see how he reacts. If he seems uneasy, you can have a passenger hold him on his lap while you drive. Another option is a specially made safety harness for dogs, which straps the dog in much like a seat belt. Do not let the dog roam loose in the vehicle—this is very dangerous! If you should stop short, your dog can be thrown and injured. If the dog starts climbing on you and pestering you while you are driving, you will not be able to concentrate on the road. It is an unsafe situation for everyone—human and canine.

ON THE ROAD

If you are going on a long road trip with your dog, be sure the hotels are dog-friendly. Many hotels do not accept dogs. Also take along some ice that can be thawed and offered to your dog if he becomes overheated. Your Pug will need to cool down, and most dogs like to lick ice.

ON-LEAD ONLY

When traveling, never let your dog off-lead in a strange area. Your dog could run away out of fear, decide to chase a passing squirrel or cat or simply want to stretch his legs without restriction—if any of these happen, you might never see your canine friend again.

For long trips, be prepared to stop to let the dog relieve himself. Take with you whatever you need to clean up after him, including some kitchen paper towels and perhaps some old rags for use should he have an accident in the car or suffer from motion sickness.

Remember never to leave your Pug in the car unattended as heat exhaustion is a very real threat for the short-faced Pug. Fortunately, the Pug is a handy size and can be carried quite readily. In warm months, leaving your Pug in the car is tantamount to inviting tragedy to your loving, little friend.

AIR TRAVEL

Air travel requires more preparation than traveling by car or rail. The dog will be required to travel in a properly sized fiberglass crate and you should always check in advance with the airline regarding specific requirements. To help the dog be at ease, put one of his favorite toys in the crate with him. Do not feed the dog for several hours before checking in, to minimize his need to relieve himself. However, certain regulations specify that water must always be made available to the dog in the crate.

Make sure your dog is properly identified and that your contact information appears on his ID tags and on his crate.

Animals travel in a different area of the plane than human passengers so every rule must be strictly adhered to so as to prevent the risk of getting separated from your dog. Inquire of your chosen airline whether your Pug can travel with you on the plane as a "carry-on." Air travel, generally, is not recommended for Pugs, as breathing difficulties can be encountered.

VACATIONS AND BOARDING

So you want to take a family vacation—and you want to include *all* members of the family. You would probably make arrangements for accommodations ahead of time anyway, but this is especially important when traveling with a dog. You do not want to make an overnight stop at the only place around for miles and find out that they do not allow dogs. Also, you do not want to reserve a place for your family without confirming that you are traveling with a dog because if it is against their policy you may not have a place to stay.

Alternatively, if you are traveling and choose not to bring your Pug, you will have to make arrangements for him while you are away. Some options are to take him to a neighbor's house to stay while you are gone, to board him at your vet's, to have a trusted neighbor stop by often or stay at your house or to bring your dog to

GOING ABROAD

For international travel, you will have to make arrangements well in advance (perhaps months), as countries' laws pertaining to bringing in animals differ. There may be health certificates and/or vaccinations that your dog will need before the trip; sometimes this has to be done within a certain time frame. When traveling to rabies-free countries, you will need to bring proof of the dog's rabies vaccination and there will likely be a quarantine period upon arrival.

Ideally your Pug can go on vacation with you. This lucky Pug is enjoying a luxury cruise on a sunny island.

a reputable boarding kennel. If you choose to board him at a kennel, you should visit in advance to see the facilities provided, how

Pugs are genuinely affectionate and loyal. You must guarantee your Pug's safety and protection by investing in proper identification for him.

clean they are and where the dogs are kept. Talk to some of the employees and see how they treat the dogs—do they spend time with the dogs, play with them, exercise them, etc.? Also find out the kennel's policy on vaccinations and what they require. This is for all of the dogs' safety, since when dogs are kept together, there is a greater risk of diseases' being passed from dog to dog.

IDENTIFICATION
Your Pug is your valued companion and friend. That is why you always keep a close eye on him and you have made sure that he cannot escape

CONSIDERATIONS ABOUT BOARDING
Will your dog be exercised at least twice a day? How often during the day will the staff keep him company? Does the kennel provide a clean and secure environment?

Likewise, if the staff asks you a lot of questions, this is a good sign. They need to know your dog's personality and temperament, health record, special requirements and what commands he has learned. Above all, follow your instincts. If you have a bad feeling about a kennel, even if a friend has recommended it, don't put your dog in its care.

from the yard or wriggle out of his collar and run away from you. However, accidents can happen and there may come a time when your dog unexpectedly gets separated from you. If this unfortunate event should occur, the first thing on your mind will be finding him. Proper identification, including an ID tag, a tattoo and possibly a microchip, will increase the chances of his being returned to you safely and quickly.

IDENTIFICATION OPTIONS

As puppies become more and more expensive, especially those puppies of high quality for showing and/or breeding, they have a greater chance of being stolen. The usual collar dog tag is, of course, easily removed. But there are two more permanent techniques that have become widely used for identification.

The puppy microchip implantation involves the injection of a small microchip, about the size of a corn kernel, under the skin of the dog. If your dog shows up at a clinic or shelter, or is offered for resale under less-than-savory circumstances, it can be positively identified by the microchip. The microchip is scanned, and a registry quickly identifies you as the owner.

Tattooing is done on various parts of the dog, from his belly to his ears. The number tattooed can be your telephone number, the dog's AKC registration number or any other number that you can easily memorize. When potential dog thieves see a tattooed dog, they usually lose interest. Both microchipping and tattooing can be done at your local veterinary clinic.

Discuss microchipping and tattooing with your vet and breeder. As well as vets, some breeders perform these services on their own premises for a reasonable fee. Be certain that the dog is then properly registered with a national database.

ID tags must be securely fastened to your dog's everyday collar.

TRAINING YOUR

PUG

Breeders commonly begin house-training before the pups are released to their new homes. Newspaper is still used by some breeders to initiate the process.

Living with an untrained dog is a lot like owning a piano that you do not know how to play—it is a nice object to look at, but it does not do much more than that to bring you pleasure. Now try taking piano lessons, and suddenly the piano comes alive and brings forth magical sounds and rhythms that set your heart singing and your body swaying.

The same is true with your Pug. Any dog is a big responsibility and if not trained sensibly may develop unacceptable behavior that annoys you or could even cause family friction.

To train your Pug, you may like to enroll in an obedience

class. Teach him good manners as you learn how and why he behaves the way he does. Find out how to communicate with your dog and how to recognize and understand his communications with you. Suddenly the dog takes on a new role in your life—he is clever, interesting, well behaved and fun to be with. He demonstrates his bond of devotion to you daily. In other words, your Pug does wonders for your ego because he constantly reminds you that you are not only his leader, you are his hero!

Those involved with teaching dog obedience and counseling owners about their dogs' behavior have discovered some interesting facts about dog ownership. For example,

training dogs when they are puppies results in the highest rate of success in developing well-mannered and well-adjusted adult dogs. Training an older dog, from six months to six years of age, can produce almost equal results, providing that the owner accepts the dog's slower rate of learning capability and is willing to work patiently to help the dog succeed at developing to his fullest potential. Unfortunately, many owners of untrained adult dogs lack the patience factor, so they do not persist until their dogs are successful at learning particular behaviors.

Training a puppy aged 10 to 16 weeks (20 weeks at the most) is like working with a dry sponge in a pool of water. The pup soaks up whatever you show him and constantly looks for more things to do and learn. At this early age, his body is not yet producing hormones, and therein lies the reason for such a high rate of success. Without hormones, he is focused on his owners and not particularly interested in investigating other places, dogs, people, etc. You are his leader: his provider of food, water, shelter and security. He latches onto you and wants to stay close. He usually will follow you from room to room, will not let you out of his sight when

PARENTAL GUIDANCE
Training a dog is a life experience. Many parents admit that much of what they know about raising children they learned from caring for their dogs. Dogs respond to love, fairness and guidance, just as children do. Become a good dog owner and you may become an even better parent.

you are outdoors with him and will respond in like manner to the people and animals you encounter. If you greet a friend warmly, he will be happy to greet the person as well. If, however, you are hesitant, even anxious, about the approach of a stranger, he will respond accordingly.

Once the puppy begins to produce hormones, his natural curiosity emerges and he begins to investigate the world around

Well-trained dogs are a pleasure to own. These two fellows have accepted the house rules and get along famously. The Pug's large housemate is a South African Boerboel.

HONOR AND OBEY

Dogs are the most honorable animals in existence. They consider another species (humans) as their own. They interface with you. You are their leader. Pugs perceive children to be on their level; their actions around small children are different from their behavior around their adult masters.

him. It is at this time when you may notice that the untrained dog begins to wander away from you and even ignore your commands to stay close. When this behavior becomes a problem, the owner has two choices: get rid of the dog or train him. It is strongly urged that you choose the latter option.

There are usually classes within a reasonable distance from the owner's home, but you also can do a lot to train your dog yourself. Sometimes there are classes available but the tuition is too costly. Whatever the circumstances, the solution to training your dog without formal obedience classes lies within the pages of this book.

This chapter is devoted to helping you train your Pug at home. If the recommended procedures are followed faithfully, you may expect positive results that will prove rewarding both to you and your dog.

Whether your new charge is a puppy or a mature adult, the methods of teaching and the techniques we use in training basic behaviors are the same. After all, no dog, whether puppy or adult, likes harsh or inhumane methods. All creatures, however, respond favorably to gentle motivational methods and sincere praise and encouragement. Now let us get started.

HOUSEBREAKING

You can train a puppy to relieve itself wherever you choose, but this must be somewhere suitable. You should bear in mind from the outset that when your puppy is old enough to go out in public places, any canine deposits must be removed at once. You will always have to carry with you a small plastic bag or "poop-scoop."

Outdoor training includes such surfaces as grass, soil and cement. Indoor training usually means training your dog to newspaper. When deciding on the surface and location that you will want your Pug to use, be sure it is going to be permanent. Training your dog to grass and then changing your mind two months later is extremely difficult for both dog and owner.

Next, choose the command you will use each and every time you want your puppy to void. "Hurry up" and "Be quick" are examples of commands commonly used by dog owners.

Get in the habit of giving the puppy your chosen relief command before you take him out. That way, when he becomes an adult, you will be able to determine if he wants to go out when you ask him. A confirmation will be signs of interest, such as wagging his tail, watching you intently, going to the door, etc.

PUPPY'S NEEDS

Puppy needs to relieve himself after play periods, after each meal, after he has been sleeping and at any time he indicates that he is looking for a place to urinate or defecate.

The urinary and intestinal tract muscles of very young puppies are not fully developed. Therefore, like human babies, puppies need to relieve themselves frequently.

Take your puppy out often— every hour for an eight-week-old, for example, and always

Reward your Pug for a job well done. Along with your praise, a treat is always much appreciated.

immediately after sleeping and eating. The older the puppy, the less often he will need to relieve himself. Finally, as a mature healthy adult, he will require only three to five relief trips per day.

HOUSING

Since the types of housing and control you provide for your puppy have a direct relationship on the success of housetraining, we consider the various aspects of both before we begin training.

Taking a new puppy home and turning him loose in your house can be compared to turning a child loose in a sports arena and telling the child that the place is all his! The sheer enormity of the place would be too much for him to handle.

Instead, offer the puppy clearly defined areas where he can play, sleep, eat and live. A room of the house where the family gathers is the most obvious choice. Puppies are social animals and need to feel a part of the pack right from the start. Hearing your voice, watching you while you are doing things and smelling you nearby are all positive reinforcers that he is now a member of your pack. Usually the living room, the kitchen or a nearby adjoining breakfast area is ideal for providing safety and security for both puppy and owner.

Within that room there

PAPER CAPER
Never line your pup's sleeping area with newspaper. Puppy litters are usually raised on newspaper and, once in your home, the puppy will immediately associate newspaper with voiding. Never put newspaper on any floor while house-training, as this will only confuse the puppy. If you are paper-training him, use paper in his designated relief area only. Finally, restrict water intake after evening meals. Offer a few licks at a time—never let a young puppy gulp water after meals.

CANINE DEVELOPMENT SCHEDULE

It is important to understand how and at what age a puppy develops into adulthood. If you are a puppy owner, consult the following Canine Development Schedule to determine the stage of development your puppy is currently experiencing. This knowledge will help you as you work with the puppy in the weeks and months ahead.

Period	Age	Characteristics
First to Third	**Birth to Seven Weeks**	Puppy needs food, sleep and warmth, and responds to simple and gentle touching. Needs mother for security and disciplining. Needs littermates for learning and interacting with other dogs. Pup learns to function within a pack and learns pack order of dominance. Begin socializing pup with adults and children for short periods. Pup begins to become aware of his environment.
Fourth	**Eight to Twelve Weeks**	Brain is fully developed. Pup needs socializing with outside world. Remove from mother and littermates. Needs to change from canine pack to human pack. Human dominance necessary. Fear period occurs between 8 and 12 weeks. Avoid fright and pain.
Fifth	**Thirteen to Sixteen Weeks**	Training and formal obedience should begin. Less association with other dogs, more with people, places, situations. Period will pass easily if you remember this is pup's change-to-adolescence time. Be firm and fair. Flight instinct prominent. Permissiveness and over-disciplining can do permanent damage. Praise for good behavior.
Juvenile	**Four to Eight Months**	Another fear period about 7 to 8 months of age. It passes quickly, but be cautious of fright and pain. Sexual maturity reached. Dominant traits established. Dog should understand sit, down, come and stay by now.

Note: These are approximate time frames. Allow for individual differences in puppies.

TAKE THE LEAD

Do not carry your dog to his relief area. Lead him there on a leash or, better yet, encourage him to follow you to the spot. If you start carrying him to his spot, you might end up doing this routine forever and your dog will have the satisfaction of having trained YOU. Be your dog's leader, not the one being led.

stretch out as well as stand up without rubbing his head on the top, yet small enough so that he cannot relieve himself at one end and sleep at the other without coming into contact with his droppings until fully trained to relieve himself outside.

Dogs are, by nature, clean animals and will not remain close to their relief areas unless forced to do so. In those cases, they then become dirty dogs and usually remain that way for life.

The designated area should contain clean bedding and a toy. Water must always be available, in a non-spill container.

CONTROL

By control, we mean helping the puppy to create a lifestyle pattern that will be compatible to that of his human pack *(you!)*. Just as we guide little children to learn our way of life, we must show the puppy when it is time to play, eat, sleep, exercise and even entertain himself.

Your puppy should always sleep in his crate. He should also learn that, during times of household confusion and excessive human activity such as at breakfast when family members are preparing for the day, he can play by himself in relative safety and comfort in

should be a smaller area that the puppy can call his own. An alcove, a wire or fiberglass dog crate or a fenced (not boarded!) corner from which he can view the activities of his new family will be fine. The size of the area or crate is the key factor here. The area must be large enough for the puppy to lie down and

his designated area. Each time you leave the puppy alone, he should understand exactly where he is to stay. Puppies are chewers. They cannot tell the difference between lamp cords, television wires, shoes, table legs, etc. Chewing into a television wire, for example, can be fatal to the puppy, while a shorted wire can start a fire in the house.

If the puppy chews on the arm of the chair when he is alone, you will probably discipline him angrily when you get home. Thus, he makes the association that your coming home means he is going to be punished. (He will not remember chewing the chair and is incapable of making the association of the discipline with his naughty deed.)

Other times of excitement,

PLAN TO PLAY

The puppy should also have regular play and exercise sessions when he is with you or a family member. Exercise for a very young puppy can consist of a short walk around the house or yard. Playing can include fetching games with a tennis ball or a special toy. (All puppies teethe and need soft things upon which to chew.) Remember to restrict play periods to indoors within his living area (the kitchen, an enclosed porch or the family room, for example) until he is completely house-trained.

A suitable crate for inside the house. Your Pug will accept his crate in no time at all and consider it his den of security.

such as family parties, etc., can be fun for the puppy, providing he can view the activities from the security of his designated area. He is not underfoot and he is not being fed all sorts of tidbits that will probably cause him stomach distress, yet he still feels a part of the fun.

PRACTICE MAKES YOUR PUG PERFECT!

- Have training lessons with your dog every day in several short segments—three to five times a day for a few minutes at a time is ideal.
- Do not have long practice sessions. The dog will become easily bored.
- Never practice when you are tired, ill, worried or in an otherwise negative mood. This will transmit to the dog and may have an adverse effect on its performance.

  Think fun, short and above all positive! End each session on a high note, rather than a failed exercise, and make sure to give a lot of praise. Enjoy the training and help your dog enjoy it, too.

SCHEDULE

A puppy should be taken to his relief area each time he is released from his designated area, after meals, after a play session and when he first awakens in the morning (at age eight weeks, this can mean 5 a.m.!). The puppy will indicate that he's ready "to go" by circling or sniffing busily—do not misinterpret these signs. For a puppy less than ten weeks of age, a routine of taking him out every hour is necessary. As the puppy grows, he will be able to wait for longer periods of time.

Keep trips to his relief area short. Stay no more than five or six minutes and then return to the house. If he goes during that time, praise him lavishly and take him indoors immediately. If he does not, but he has an accident when you go back indoors, pick him up immediately, say "No! No!" and return to his relief area. Wait a few minutes, then return to the house again. Never hit a puppy or rub his face in urine or excrement when he has had an accident!

Once indoors, put the puppy in his crate until you have had time to clean up his accident. Then release him to the family area and watch him more closely than before. Chances are, his accident was a result of your not picking up his signal or waiting too long before offering him the opportunity to relieve himself. Never hold a grudge against the puppy for accidents.

Let the puppy learn that going outdoors means it is time to relieve himself, not to play. Once trained, he will be able to play indoors and out and still differentiate between the times for play versus the times for relief.

Help him develop regular hours for naps, being alone, playing by himself and just resting, all in his crate. Encourage him to entertain himself while you are busy with your activities. Let him learn that having you near is comforting, but it is not your main purpose in life to provide him with undivided attention.

Each time you put a puppy in his own area, use the same command, whatever suits best. Soon he will run to his crate or special area when he hears you say those words.

Crate training provides safety for you, the puppy and the home. It also provides the puppy with a feeling of security, and that helps the puppy achieve self-confidence and clean habits.

Remember that one of the primary ingredients in house-training your puppy is control.

THE CLEAN LIFE

By providing sleeping and resting quarters that fit the dog, and offering frequent opportunities to relieve himself outside his quarters, the puppy quickly learns that the outdoors (or the newspaper if you are training him to paper) is the place to go when he needs to urinate or defecate. It also reinforces his innate desire to keep his sleeping quarters clean. This, in turn, helps develop the muscle control that will eventually produce a dog with clean living habits. The benefits of crate training long outlast the efforts involved in accustoming the pup to his new den.

Regardless of your lifestyle, there will always be occasions when you will need to have a place where your dog can stay and be happy and safe. Crate training is the answer for now and in the future.

In conclusion, a few key elements are really all you need for a successful house-training method—consistency, frequency, praise, control and supervision. By following these procedures with a normal, healthy puppy, you and the puppy soon will be ready to

THE SUCCESS METHOD

Success that comes by luck is usually short-lived. Success that comes by well-thought-out proven methods is often more easily achieved and permanent. This is the Success Method. It is designed to give you, the puppy owner, a simple yet proven way to help your puppy develop clean living habits and a feeling of security in his new environment.

6 Steps to Successful Crate Training

1 Tell the puppy "Crate time!" and place him in the crate with a small treat (a piece of cheese or half of a biscuit). Let him stay in the crate for five minutes while you are in the same room. Then release him and praise lavishly. Never release him when he is fussing. Wait until he is quiet before you let him out.

2 Repeat Step 1 several times a day.

3 The next day, place the puppy in the crate as before. Let him stay there for ten minutes. Do this several times.

4 Continue building time in five-minute increments until the puppy stays in his crate for 30 minutes with you in the room. Always take him to his relief area after prolonged periods in his crate.

5 Now go back to Step 1 and let the puppy stay in his crate for five minutes, this time while you are out of the room.

6 Once again, build crate time in five-minute increments with you out of the room. When the puppy will stay willingly in his crate (he may even fall asleep!) for 30 minutes with you out of the room, he will be ready to stay in it for several hours at a time.

move on to a clean and rewarding life together.

ROLES OF DISCIPLINE, REWARD AND PUNISHMENT

Discipline, training one to act in accordance with rules, brings order to life. It is as simple as that. Without discipline, particularly in a group society, chaos reigns supreme and the group will eventually perish. Humans and canines are social animals and need some form of discipline in order to function effectively. They must procure food, protect their home base and their young and reproduce to keep the species going.

If there were no discipline

HOW MANY TIMES A DAY?

AGE	RELIEF TRIPS
To 14 weeks	10
14–22 weeks	8
22–32 weeks	6
Adulthood (dog stops growing)	4

These are estimates, of course, but they are a guide to the *minimum* opportunities a dog should have each day to relieve itself.

Crate training is the best lesson you will ever teach your Pug. In addition to housebreaking, crate training proves helpful with chewing problems and many other behavior issues that may arise.

in the lives of social animals, they would eventually die from starvation and/or predation by other stronger animals.

In the case of domestic canines, dogs need discipline in their lives in order to understand how their pack (you and other family members) functions and how they must act in order to survive.

A large humane society in a highly populated area recently

COMMAND STANCE

Stand up straight and authoritatively when giving your dog commands. Do not issue commands when lying on the floor or lying on your back on the sofa. If you are on your hands and knees when you give a command, your dog will think you are positioning yourself to play and may not be as attentive to you.

surveyed dog owners regarding their satisfaction with their relationships with their dogs. People who had trained their dogs were 75% more satisfied with their pets than those who had never trained their dogs.

Dr. Edward Thorndike, a psychologist, established *Thorndike's Theory of Learning*, which states that a behavior that results in a pleasant event tends to be repeated. A behavior that results in an unpleasant event tends not to be repeated. It is this theory on which training methods are based today. For example, if you manipulate a dog to perform a specific behavior and reward him for doing it, he is likely to do it again because he enjoyed the end result.

Occasionally, punishment, a penalty inflicted for an offense, is necessary. The best type of punishment often comes from an outside source. For example, a child is told not to touch the stove because he may get burned. He disobeys and touches the stove. In doing so, he receives a burn. From that time on, he respects the heat of the stove and avoids contact with it. Therefore, a behavior that results in an unpleasant event tends not to be repeated.

An example of a dog learning the hard way is the dog who chases the house cat. He is told many times to leave the cat alone, yet he persists in teasing the cat. Then, one day he begins chasing the cat, but the cat turns and swipes a claw across the dog's face, leaving him with a gash on his nose. The end result is the dog stops chasing the cat.

TRAINING EQUIPMENT

COLLAR AND LEAD
For a Pug, the collar and lead that you use for training must be one with which you are easily able to work, not too heavy for the dog and perfectly safe.

TREATS
Have a bag of treats on hand. Something nutritious and easy to swallow works best. Use a soft treat, a chunk of cheese or a piece of cooked chicken rather than a dry biscuit. By the time the dog has finished chewing a dry treat, he will forget why he is being rewarded in the first place! Using food rewards will not teach a dog to beg at the table—the only way to teach a dog to beg at the table is to give him food from the table. In training, rewarding the dog with a food treat will help him associate praise and the treats with learning new behaviors that obviously please his owner.

TRAINING BEGINS: ASK THE DOG A QUESTION
In order to teach your dog anything, you must first get his attention. After all, he cannot learn anything if he is distracted and looking away

LANGUAGE BARRIER
Dogs do not understand our language. They can be trained to react to a certain sound, at a certain volume. If you say "No, Oliver" in a very soft, pleasant voice, it will not have the same meaning as "No, Oliver!!" when you raise your voice. You should never use the dog's name during a reprimand, just the command NO!!

Since dogs don't understand words, comics often train dogs to commands with opposite meaning. Thus, when the comic commands his dog to sit, the dog will stand up, and vice versa.

from you with his mind on something else.

To get his attention, ask him, "School?" and immediately walk over to him and give him a treat as you tell him "Good dog." Wait a minute or two and repeat the routine, this time with a treat in your hand as you approach within a foot of the dog. Do not go directly to him, but stop about a foot short of him and hold out the treat as you ask, "School?" He will see you approaching with a treat in your hand and most likely begin walking toward you. As you meet, give him the treat and praise again.

The third time, ask the question, have a treat in your hand and walk only a short distance toward the dog so that he must walk almost all the way to you. As he reaches you, give

You should accustom your Pug to a loose-fitting, light-weight collar as quickly as possible after you acquire him. Check the snugness of the collar every day since your puppy will grow quickly.

him the treat and praise again.

By this time, the dog will probably be getting the idea that if he pays attention to you, especially when you ask that question, it will pay off in treats and enjoyable activities for him. In other words, he learns that "school" means doing great things with you that are fun and result in positive attention for him.

Remember that the dog does not understand your verbal language; he only recognizes sounds. Your question translates to a series of sounds for him, and those sounds become the signal to go to you and pay attention; if he does, he will get to interact with you plus receive treats and praise.

THE BASIC COMMANDS

TEACHING SIT

Now that you have the dog's attention, attach his lead and hold it in your left hand and a food treat in your right. Place your food hand at the dog's nose and let him lick the treat but not take it from you. Say "Sit" and slowly raise your food hand from in front of the dog's nose up over his head so that he is looking at the ceiling. As he bends his head upward, he will have to bend his knees to maintain his balance. As he bends his knees, he will assume a sit position. At that point, release the food treat and praise lavishly with comments such as "Good dog! Good sit!," etc. Remember to always praise enthusiastically, because dogs relish verbal praise from their owners and feel so proud of themselves whenever they accomplish a behavior.

You will not use food forever in getting the dog to obey your commands. Food is only used to teach new behaviors, and once the dog knows what you want when you give a specific command, you will wean him off the food treats but still maintain the verbal praise. After all, you will always have your voice with you, and there will be many times when you have no food rewards but expect the dog to obey.

The sit command makes the ideal starting place for teaching the basic commands. As your training progresses, you can always reinforce the sit command at the end of every lesson so that you end on a positive note.

TEACHING DOWN

Teaching the down exercise is easy when you understand how the dog perceives the down position, and it is very difficult when you do not. Dogs perceive the down position as a submissive one; therefore, teaching the down exercise using a forceful method can sometimes make the dog develop such a fear of the down that he either runs away when you say "Down" or

ATTENTION!
Your dog is actually training you at the same time you are training him. Dogs do things to get attention. They usually repeat whatever succeeds in getting your attention.

DOUBLE JEOPARDY

A dog in jeopardy never lies down. He stays alert on his feet because instinct tells him that he may have to run away or fight for his survival. Therefore, if a dog feels threatened or anxious, he will not lie down. Consequently, it is important to keep the dog calm and relaxed as he learns the down exercise.

he attempts to snap at the person who tries to force him down.

Have the dog sit close alongside your left leg, facing in the same direction as you are. Hold the lead in your left hand and a food treat in your right. Now place your left hand lightly on the top of the dog's shoulders where they meet above the spinal cord. Do not push down on the dog's shoulders; simply rest your left hand there so you can guide the dog to lie down close to your left leg rather than to swing away from your side when he drops.

Now place the food hand at the dog's nose, say "Down" very softly (almost a whisper) and slowly lower the food hand to the dog's front feet. When the food hand reaches the floor, begin moving it forward along the floor in front of the dog. Keep talking softly to the dog, saying things like, "Do you want this treat? You can do this, good dog." Your reassuring tone of voice will help calm the dog as he tries to follow the food hand in order to get the treat.

When the dog's elbows touch the floor, release the food and praise softly. Try to get the dog to maintain that down position for several seconds before you let him sit up again. The goal here is to get the dog

SAFETY FIRST

While it may seem that the most important things to your dog are eating, sleeping and chewing the upholstery on your furniture, his first concern is actually safety. The domesticated dogs we keep as companions have the same pack instinct as their ancestors who ran free thousands of years ago. Because of this pack instinct, your dog wants to know that he and his pack are not in danger of being harmed, and that his pack has a strong, capable leader. You must establish yourself as the leader early on in your relationship. That way your dog will trust that you will take care of him and the pack, and he will accept your commands without question.

in your left hand. Have a food treat in your right hand and place your food hand at the dog's nose. Say "Stay" and step out on your right foot to stand directly in front of the dog, toe to toe, as he licks and nibbles the treat. Be sure to keep his head facing upward to maintain the sit position. Count to five and then swing around to stand next to the dog again with him on your left. As soon as you get back to the original position, release the food and praise lavishly.

To teach the down/stay, do the down as previously

With practice and consistency, your Pug will be able to understand commands by voice and by hand signal. This Pug has mastered the down command.

to settle down and not feel threatened in the down position.

TEACHING STAY

It is easy to teach the dog to stay in either a sit or a down position. Again, we use food and praise during the teaching process as we help the dog to understand exactly what it is that we are expecting him to do.

To teach the sit/stay, start with the dog sitting on your left side as before and hold the lead

CONSISTENCY PAYS OFF

Dogs need consistency in their feeding schedule, exercise and relief visits, and in the verbal commands you use. If you use "Stay" on Monday and "Stay here, please" on Tuesday, you will confuse your dog. Don't demand perfect behavior during training sessions and then let him have the run of the house the rest of the day. Above all, lavish praise on your pet consistently every time he does something right. The more he feels he is pleasing you, the more willing he will be to learn.

described. As soon as the dog lies down, say "Stay" and step out on your right foot just as you did in the sit/stay. Count to five and then return to stand beside the dog with him on your left side. Release the treat and praise as always.

Within a week or ten days, you can begin to add a bit of distance between you and your dog when you leave him. When you do, use your left hand open with the palm facing the dog as a stay signal, much the same as the hand signal a police officer uses to stop traffic at an intersection. Hold the food treat in your right hand as before, but this time the food is not touching the dog's nose. He will watch the food hand and quickly learn that he is going to get that treat as

soon as you return to his side.

When you can stand 1 yard away from your dog for 30 seconds, you can then begin building time and distance in both stays. Eventually, the dog can be expected to remain in the stay position for prolonged periods of time until you return to him or call him to you. Always praise lavishly when he stays.

TEACHING COME
If you make teaching "come" an exciting experience, you should never have a "student" that does not love the game or that fails to come when called. The secret, it seems, is never to use the word "come."

At times when an owner most wants his dog to come when called, the owner is likely to be upset or anxious and he allows these feelings to come through in the tone of his voice when he calls his dog. Hearing that desperation in his owner's voice, the dog fears the results of going to him and therefore either disobeys outright or runs in the opposite direction. The secret, therefore, is to teach the dog a game and, when you want him to come to you, simply play the game. It is practically a no-fail solution!

To begin, have several members of your family take a few food treats and each go into a different room in the house. Take turns calling the dog, and each person should celebrate the dog's finding him with a treat and lots of happy praise. When a person calls the dog, he is actually inviting the dog to find him and get a treat as a reward for "winning."

A few turns of the "Where are you?" game and the dog will understand that everyone is playing the game and that each person has a big celebration awaiting his success at locating him or her. Once he learns to love the game, simply

"COME" ... BACK
Never call your dog to come to you for a correction or scold him when he reaches you. That is the quickest way to turn a "Come" command into "Go away fast!" Dogs think only in the present tense, and your dog will connect the scolding with coming to you, not with the misbehavior of a few moments earlier.

calling out "Where are you?" will bring him running from wherever he is when he hears that all-important question.

"Where are you?" works wonders on a mischievous Pug! Since all dogs can be a bit stubborn at times, this game proves to work on most breeds of dog.

WEANING THE "TREAT HOG"

If you have trained your dog by rewarding him with a treat each time he performs a command, he may soon decide that without the treat, he won't obey. The best way to fix this problem is to start asking your dog to do certain commands twice before being rewarded. Slowly increase the number of commands and then vary the number: three sits and a treat one day, five sits for a biscuit the next day, etc. Your dog will soon realize that there is no set number of sits before he gets his reward and he'll likely do it the first time you ask hoping to be rewarded. Whenever there's the chance of a tasty morsel, your Pug will remain attentive and ready to respond.

The come command is recognized as one of the most important things to teach a dog, but there are trainers who work with thousands of dogs and never teach the actual word "come." Yet these dogs will race to respond to a person who uses the dog's name followed by "Where are you?" For example, a woman has a 12-year-old companion dog who went blind, but who never fails to locate her owner when asked, "Where are you?"

Children, in particular, love to play this game with their dogs. Children can hide in smaller places like a shower or bathtub, behind a bed or under a table. The dog needs to work a little bit harder to find these hiding places, but when he does he loves to celebrate with a treat and a tussle with a favorite youngster.

TEACHING HEEL

Heeling means that the dog walks beside the owner without pulling. It takes time and patience on the owner's part to succeed at teaching the dog that he (the owner) will not proceed unless the dog is walking calmly beside him. Pulling out ahead on the lead is definitely not acceptable.

Begin by holding the lead in your left hand as the dog sits beside your left leg. Move the loop end of the lead to your right hand but keep your left hand short on the lead so it keeps the dog in close next to you.

Say "Heel" and step forward on your left foot. Keep the dog close to you and take three steps. Stop and have the dog sit next to you in what we now call the heel position. Praise verbally, but do not touch the dog. Hesitate a moment and begin again with "Heel," taking three steps and stopping, at which point the dog is told to sit again.

Your goal here is to have the dog walk those three steps without pulling on the lead. Once he will walk calmly beside you for three steps without pulling, increase the number of steps you take to five. When he will walk politely beside you while you take five steps, you can increase the length of your walk to ten steps. Keep increasing the length of your stroll until the dog will walk quietly beside you without pulling as long as you want him to heel. When you stop heeling, indicate to the dog that the exercise is over by verbally praising as you pet him and say "OK, good dog." The "OK" is used as a release word, meaning that the exercise is finished and the dog is free to relax.

TUG OF WALK?
If you begin teaching the heel by taking long walks and letting the dog pull you along, he misinterprets this action as an acceptable form of taking a walk. When you pull back on the lead to counteract his pulling, he reads that tug as a signal to pull even harder! Remember *you* are the one who sets the pace.

If you are dealing with a dog who insists on pulling you around, simply "put on your brakes" and stand your ground until the dog realizes that the two of you are not going anywhere until he is beside you and moving at your pace, not his. It may take some time just standing there to convince the dog that you are the leader and you will be the one to decide on the direction and speed of your travel.

Each time the dog looks up at you or slows down to give a slack lead between the two of you, quietly praise him and say, "Good heel. Good dog." Eventually, the dog will begin to respond and within a few days he will be walking politely beside you without pulling on the lead. At first, the training sessions should be kept short and very positive; soon the dog will be able to walk nicely with you for increasingly longer distances. Remember also to give the dog free time and the opportunity to run and play when you have finished heel practice.

WEANING OFF FOOD IN TRAINING

Food is used in training new behaviors. Once the dog understands what behavior goes with a specific command, it is time to start weaning him off the food treats. At first, give a treat after each exercise. Then, start to give a treat only after every other exercise. Mix up the times when you offer a food reward and the times when you only offer praise so that the dog will never know when he is going to receive both food and praise and when he is going to receive only praise. This is called a variable ratio reward system and it proves successful because there is always the chance that the owner will produce a treat, so the dog never stops trying for that reward. No matter what, *always* give verbal praise.

OBEDIENCE CLASSES

It is a good idea to enroll in an obedience class if one is available in your area. If yours is a show dog, showing classes would be more appropriate. Many areas have dog clubs that offer basic obedience training as well as preparatory classes for obedience competition. There are also local dog trainers who offer similar classes.

At obedience trials, dogs can earn titles at various levels of competition. The beginning levels of competition include basic behaviors such as sit, down, heel, etc. The more advanced levels of competition include jumping, retrieving, scent discrimination and signal work. The advanced levels require a dog and owner to put a lot of time and effort into their training and the titles that can be earned at these levels of competition are very prestigious.

OTHER ACTIVITIES FOR LIFE

Whether a dog is trained in the structured environment of a class or alone with his owner at home,

providing an outlet for his energy.

If you are interested in participating in organized competition with your Pug, there are activities other than obedience in which you and your dog can become involved.

Agility is a popular sport where dogs run through an obstacle course that includes various jumps, tunnels and other exercises to test the dog's speed and coordination. Pugs are particularly fond of the tunnel since they fit through the obstacle with little effort. Jumps, on the other hand, are the Pug's least favorite obstacles. The owners run beside their dogs to give commands and to guide them through the course. Although competitive, the focus is on fun—it's fun to do, fun to watch and great exercise.

Some Pugs are very social creatures and have their own tea parties and garden parties— special delicate little sandwiches are not unknown at these! Pugs apparently also adore dressing up, so fancy dress parties are popular too. Pugs are proud members of the Toy Group and don't mind entertaining an adoring crowd.

Another popular activity for our breed are Pug races. Toy monkeys (the "jockeys") are strapped to Pugs' backs, and the Pugs race against each other—to the evident delight of all concerned!

Daily practice is key to keeping your Pug's obedience training sharp and consistent. Never take training for granted. It requires commitment and persistence.

there are many activities that can bring fun and rewards to both owner and dog once they have mastered basic control. Here are some of the many possible activities for you to try with your Pug.

Teaching the dog to help out around the home, in the yard or on the farm provides great satisfaction to both dog and owner. In addition, the dog's help makes life a little easier for his owner and raises his stature as a valued companion to his family. It helps give the dog a purpose by occupying his mind and

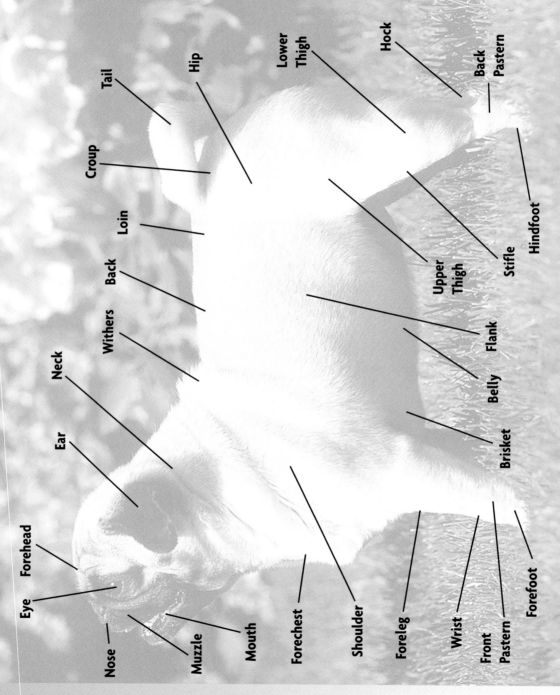

Physical Structure of the Pug

PUG

Dogs suffer from many of the same physical illnesses as people. They might even share many of the same psychological problems. Since people usually know more about human diseases than canine maladies, many of the terms used in this chapter will be familiar but not necessarily those used by veterinarians. We will use the term *x-ray*, instead of the more acceptable term *radiograph*. We will also use the familiar term *symptoms* even though dogs don't have symptoms, which are verbal descriptions of the patient's feelings; dogs have *clinical signs*. Since dogs can't speak, we have to look for clinical signs...but we still use the term *symptoms* in this book.

As a general rule, medicine is *practiced*. That term is not arbitrary. Medicine is a constantly changing art as we learn more and more about genetics, electronic aids (like CAT scans and MRIs) and daily laboratory advances. There are many dog maladies, like canine hip dysplasia, which are not universally treated in the same manner. Some veterinarians opt for surgery more often than others do.

Before you buy your Pug, meet and interview the veterinarians in your area. Take everything into consideration; discuss background, specialties, fees, emergency policies, etc.

SELECTING A QUALIFIED VET

Your selection of a veterinarian should be based upon ability and personality as well as upon convenience to your home. You want a vet who is close because you might have emergencies or need to make multiple visits for treatments. You want a vet who has services that you might require such as tattooing and boarding, as well as sophisticated pet supplies and a good reputation for ability and responsiveness. There is nothing more frustrating than having to wait a day or more to get a response from your veterinarian.

All veterinarians are licensed and their diplomas and/or certificates should be displayed in their

1. Esophagus
2. Lungs
3. Gall Bladder
4. Liver
5. Kidney
6. Stomach
7. Intestines
8. Urinary Bladder

Internal Organs of the Pug

waiting rooms. There are, however, many veterinary specialties that usually require further studies and internships. There are specialists in heart problems (veterinary cardiologists), skin problems (veterinary dermatologists), teeth and gum problems (veterinary dentists), eye problems (veterinary ophthalmologists) and x-rays (veterinary radiologists), as well as vets who have specialities in bones, muscles or other organs. Most veterinarians do routine surgery such as neutering, stitching up wounds and docking tails for those breeds in which such is required for show purposes.

When the problem affecting your dog is serious, it is not unusual or impudent to get another medical opinion, although it is best to advise the vets concerned about this. You might also want to compare costs among several veterinarians. Sophisticated health care and veterinary services can be very costly. It is not infrequent that important decisions are based upon financial considerations.

PREVENTATIVE MEDICINE

It is much easier, less costly and more effective to practice preventative medicine than to fight bouts of illness and disease. Properly bred puppies come from parents that were selected based upon their genetic disease profile. Their

Breakdown of Veterinary Income by Category

2%	Dentistry
4%	Radiology
12%	Surgery
15%	Vaccinations
19%	Laboratory
23%	Examinations
25%	Medicines

A typical vet's income, categorized according to services performed. This survey dealt with small-animal (pets) practices.

mothers should have been vaccinated, free of all internal and external parasites and properly nourished. For these reasons, a visit to the veterinarian who cared for the dam is recommended. The dam can pass on disease resistance to her puppies, which can last for eight to ten weeks. She can also pass on parasites and many infections. That's why it is helpful for you to know about the dam's health background.

VACCINATION SCHEDULING

Most vaccinations are given by injection and should only be done by a veterinarian. Both he and you should keep a record of the date of the injection, the identification of the vaccine and the amount given. Some vets give a first vaccination at six weeks, but most dog breeders prefer the course not to commence until

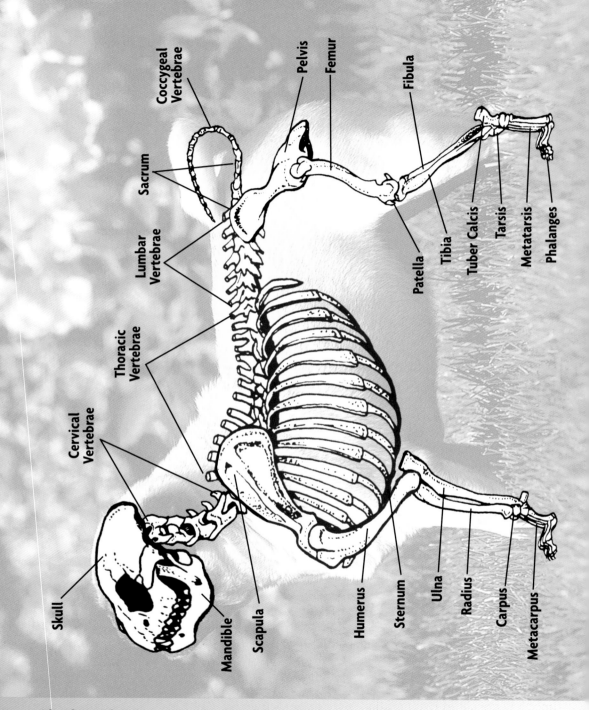

Coccygeal
Vertebrae

Pelvis

Femur

Fibula

Sacrum

Lumbar
Vertebrae

Patella

Tibia

Tuber Calcis

Tarsis

Metatarsis

Phalanges

Thoracic
Vertebrae

Cervical
Vertebrae

Skull

Mandible

Scapula

Humerus

Sternum

Ulna

Radius

Carpus

Metacarpus

Skeletal Structure of the Pug

about eight weeks because of negating any antibodies passed on by the dam. The vaccination scheduling is usually based on a 15-day cycle. You must take your vet's advice regarding when to vaccinate, as this may differ according to the vaccine used. Most vaccinations immunize your puppy against viruses.

The usual vaccines contain immunizing doses of several different viruses such as distemper, parvovirus, parainfluenza and hepatitis, although some veterinarians recommend separate vaccines for each disease. There are other vaccines available when the puppy is at risk. You should rely upon professional advice. This is especially true for the booster-shot program. Most vaccination programs require a booster when the puppy is a year old and once a year thereafter. In some cases, circumstances may require more or less frequent immunizations. Canine cough, more formally known as tracheobronchitis, is treated with a vaccine that is sprayed into the dog's nostrils. Canine cough is usually included in routine vaccinations, but this is often not so effective as for other major diseases.

WEANING TO FIVE MONTHS OLD

Puppies should be weaned by the time they are about two months old. A puppy that remains for at

VACCINATIONS FIRST

Your vet will recommend that your puppy be fully vaccinated before you take him outside. There are airborne diseases, parasite eggs in the grass and visits from other dogs, which are the most harmful reservoir of pathogenic organisms, as everything they have can be transmitted to your Pug.

least eight weeks with its mother and littermates usually adapts better to other dogs and people later in its life.

Some new owners have their puppy examined by a veterinarian immediately, which is a good idea. Vaccination programs usually begin when the puppy is very young.

The puppy will have its teeth examined and have its skeletal conformation and general health

HEALTH AND VACCINATION SCHEDULE

Age in Weeks:	6th	8th	10th	12th	14th	16th	20-24th	52nd
Worm Control	✔	✔	✔	✔	✔	✔	✔	
Neutering							✔	
Heartworm		✔		✔		✔	✔	
Parvovirus	✔		✔		✔		✔	✔
Distemper		✔		✔		✔		✔
Hepatitis		✔		✔		✔		✔
Leptospirosis								✔
Parainfluenza	✔		✔		✔			✔
Dental Examination		✔					✔	✔
Complete Physical		✔					✔	✔
Coronavirus				✔			✔	✔
Canine Cough	✔							
Hip Dysplasia							✔	
Rabies							✔	

Vaccinations are not instantly effective. It takes about two weeks for the dog's immune system to develop antibodies. Most vaccinations require annual booster shots. Your vet should guide you in this regard.

checked prior to certification by the veterinarian. Pug puppies may have problems with their kneecaps, cataracts and other eye problems, heart murmurs and undescended testicles. They may also have personality problems and your veterinarian might have training in temperament testing.

FIVE TO TWELVE MONTHS OF AGE
Unless you intend to breed or show your dog, neutering the puppy at six months of age is recommended. Discuss this with your veterinarian. Neutering (for males) and spaying (for females) have proven to be extremely beneficial to both male and female puppies. Besides eliminating the possibility of pregnancy and pyometra in bitches and testicular cancer in males, it inhibits (but does not prevent) breast cancer in bitches and prostate cancer in male dogs.

Your veterinarian should provide your puppy with a thorough dental evaluation at six months of age, ascertaining whether all permanent teeth have erupted properly. A home dental-care regimen should be initiated at six months, including brushing weekly and providing good dental devices (such as nylon bones). Regular dental care promotes healthy teeth, fresh breath and a longer life.

OVER ONE YEAR OF AGE
Once a year, your grown dog should visit the vet for an examination and vaccination boosters, if needed. Some vets recommend blood tests, thyroid level check and dental evaluation to accompany these annual visits.

A thorough clinical evaluation by the vet can provide critical background information for your dog. Blood tests are often performed at one year of age, and dental examinations around the third or fourth birthday. In the long run, quality preventative care for your pet can save money, teeth and lives.

SKIN PROBLEMS IN PUGS
Veterinarians are consulted by dog owners for skin problems more than any other group of diseases or maladies. Dogs' skin is

DISEASE REFERENCE CHART

	What is it?	What causes it?	Symptoms
Leptospirosis	Severe disease that affects the internal organs; can be spread to people.	A bacterium, which is often carried by rodents, that enters through mucous membranes and spreads quickly throughout the body.	Range from fever, vomiting and loss of appetite in less severe cases to shock, irreversible kidney damage and possibly death in most severe cases.
Rabies	Potentially deadly virus that infects warm-blooded mammals.	Bite from a carrier of the virus, mainly wild animals.	1st stage: dog exhibits change in behavior, fear. 2nd stage: dog's behavior becomes more aggressive. 3rd stage: loss of coordination, trouble with bodily functions.
Parvovirus	Highly contagious virus, potentially deadly.	Ingestion of the virus, which is usually spread through the feces of infected dogs.	Most common: severe diarrhea. Also vomiting, fatigue, lack of appetite.
Canine cough	Contagious respiratory infection.	Combination of types of bacteria and virus. Most common: *Bordetella bronchiseptica* bacteria and parainfluenza virus.	Chronic cough.
Distemper	Disease primarily affecting respiratory and nervous system.	Virus that is related to the human measles virus.	Mild symptoms such as fever, lack of appetite and mucus secretion progress to evidence of brain damage, "hard pad."
Hepatitis	Virus primarily affecting the liver.	Canine adenovirus type I (CAV-1). Enters system when dog breathes in particles.	Lesser symptoms include listlessness, diarrhea, vomiting. More severe symptoms include "blue-eye" (clumps of virus in eye).
Coronavirus	Virus resulting in digestive problems.	Virus is spread through infected dog's feces.	Stomach upset evidenced by lack of appetite, vomiting, diarrhea.

Normal hairs of a dog enlarged 200 times original size. The cuticle (outer covering) is clean and healthy. Unlike human hair that grows from the base, a dog's hair also grows from the end, as shown in the inset.

almost as sensitive as human skin and both suffer almost the same ailments (though the occurrence of acne in dogs is rare!). For this reason, veterinary dermatology has developed into a specialty practiced by many veterinarians.

Since many skin problems have visual symptoms that are almost identical, it requires the skill of an experienced veterinary dermatologist to identify and cure many of the more severe skin disorders. Pet shops sell many treatments for skin problems, but most of the treatments are directed at symptoms and not the underlying problem(s). If your dog is suffering from a skin disorder, you should seek professional assistance as quickly as possible. As with all diseases, the earlier a problem is identified and treated, the better the chances are that the cure will be successful.

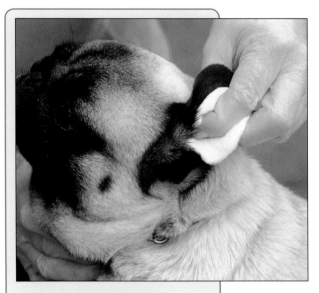

MANY KINDS OF EARS
Not every dog's ears are the same. Ears that are open to the air are healthier than ears with poor air circulation. Sometimes a dog can have two differently shaped ears. You should not probe inside your dog's ears. Only clean that which is accessible with a cotton ball.

HEREDITARY SKIN DISORDERS

Veterinary dermatologists are currently researching a number of skin disorders that are believed to have a hereditary basis. These inherited diseases are transmitted by both parents, who appear (phenotypically) normal but have a recessive gene for the disease, meaning that they carry, but are not affected by, the disease. These diseases pose serious problems to breeders because in some instances there is no method of identifying carriers. Often the secondary diseases associated with these skin conditions are even more debilitating than the disorder itself, including cancers and respiratory problems, some of which can be lethal.

Among the hereditary skin disorders, for which the mode of inheritance is known, are acroder-

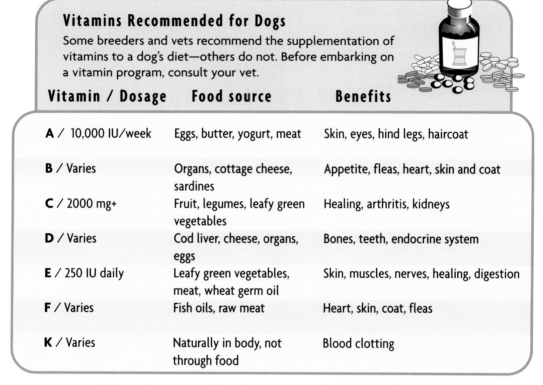

Vitamins Recommended for Dogs

Some breeders and vets recommend the supplementation of vitamins to a dog's diet—others do not. Before embarking on a vitamin program, consult your vet.

Vitamin / Dosage	Food source	Benefits
A / 10,000 IU/week	Eggs, butter, yogurt, meat	Skin, eyes, hind legs, haircoat
B / Varies	Organs, cottage cheese, sardines	Appetite, fleas, heart, skin and coat
C / 2000 mg+	Fruit, legumes, leafy green vegetables	Healing, arthritis, kidneys
D / Varies	Cod liver, cheese, organs, eggs	Bones, teeth, endocrine system
E / 250 IU daily	Leafy green vegetables, meat, wheat germ oil	Skin, muscles, nerves, healing, digestion
F / Varies	Fish oils, raw meat	Heart, skin, coat, fleas
K / Varies	Naturally in body, not through food	Blood clotting

matitis, cutaneous asthenia (Ehlers-Danlos syndrome), sebaceous adenitis, cyclic hematopoiesis, dermatomyositis, IgA deficiency, color dilution alopecia and nodular dermatofibrosis. Some of these disorders are limited to one or two breeds and others affect a large number of breeds. All inherited diseases must be diagnosed and treated by a veterinary specialist.

FLEA AND INSECT BITES

Many Pugs are prone to be allergic to insect bites, making flea prevention even more important in this sensitive breed. Flea bites itch, erupt and may even become infected. Dogs have the same reaction to ticks and mites as they do to fleas. When an insect lands on you, you have the chance to whisk it away with your hand. Unfortunately, when your dog is bitten by a flea, tick or mite, it can only scratch it away or bite it. By the time the dog has been bitten, the parasite has done some of its damage. It may also have laid eggs to cause further problems in the near future. The itching from parasite bites is probably due to the saliva injected into the site when the parasite sucks the dog's blood.

AUTO-IMMUNE SKIN CONDITIONS
Auto-immune skin conditions are commonly referred to as being allergic to yourself, while allergies are usually inflammatory reactions to an outside stimulus.

Auto-immune diseases cause serious damage to the tissues that are involved.

The best known auto-immune disease is lupus, which affects people as well as dogs. The symptoms are variable and may affect the kidneys, bones, blood chemistry and skin. It can be fatal to both dogs and humans, though it is not thought to be transmis-

12 Ways to Prevent Bloat

Gastric torsion or bloat is a preventable killer of dogs. Although bloat affects more large dogs and deep-chested dogs than any other dogs, Pugs are also at risk. Bloat can be defined as the rapid accumulation of air in the stomach, causing it to twist or flip over, thereby blocking the entrance and exit. A dog suffering from bloat experiences acute pain and is unable to release the gas. Here are some ways to prevent this life-threatening condition.

- Do not provide water at mealtimes, especially for dogs that commonly drink large amounts of water.
- Keep your dog at his proper weight. Avoid overfeeding.
- Limit exercise one hour before and after mealtime.
- Avoid stressful or vigorous exercise altogether.
- Provide antacids for any dog with audible stomach motions (borborygmus) or flatulence.
- Feed two or three smaller meals instead of one large meal per day.
- Serve your dog's food on a bowl stand so that he does not have to crane his neck to eat. For the Pug, the stand may or may not be effective.

- Be certain that mealtime is a non-stressful time. Feed the dog alone, where he is not competing with a canine or feline housemate for his bowl. Feeding the dog in his crate is an excellent solution.
- For the big gulper, place large toys in the dog's bowl so that he cannot gulp his portions.
- Discuss bloat prevention and preventative surgical methods with your veterinarian.
- If changing your dog's diet, do so gradually.
- Recognize the symptoms of bloat, as time is of the essence. Symptoms include pacing, whining, retching (with no result), groaning and obvious discomfort.

DENTAL HEALTH

A dental examination is in order when the dog is between six months and one year of age so that any permanent teeth that have erupted incorrectly can be corrected. It is important to begin a brushing routine when the puppy is young. Use a toothbrush made for dogs and specially formulated canine toothpaste. Durable nylon and safe edible chews should be a part of your puppy's arsenal for good health, good teeth and pleasant breath. The vast majority of dogs three to four years old and older has diseases of the gums from lack of dental attention. Using the various types of dental chews can be very effective in controlling dental plaque.

sible. It is usually successfully treated with cortisone, prednisone or a similar corticosteroid, but extensive use of these drugs can have harmful side effects.

AIRBORNE ALLERGIES

Just as humans have hay fever, rose fever and other fevers from which they suffer during the pollinating season, many dogs suffer from the same allergies. When the pollen count is high, your dog might suffer but don't expect him to sneeze and have a runny nose as humans. Dogs react to pollen allergies the same

way they react to fleas—they scratch and bite themselves.

Dogs, like humans, can be tested for allergens. Discuss the testing with your veterinary dermatologist.

FOOD PROBLEMS

FOOD ALLERGIES

Dogs are allergic to many foods that are best-sellers and highly recommended by breeders and veterinarians. Changing the brand of food that you buy may not eliminate the problem if the element to which the dog is allergic is contained in the new brand.

Recognizing a food allergy is difficult. Humans vomit or have rashes when they eat a food to which they are allergic. Dogs neither vomit nor (usually) develop a rash. They react in the same manner as they do to an airborne or flea allergy; they itch, scratch and bite, thus making the diagnosis extremely difficult. While pollen allergies and parasite bites are usually seasonal, food allergies are year-round problems.

FOOD INTOLERANCE

Food intolerance is the inability of the dog to completely digest certain foods. Puppies that may have done very well on their mother's milk may not do well on cow's milk. The result of this food intolerance may be loose bowels, passing gas and stomach pains. These are the only obvious symptoms of food intolerance, and that makes diagnosis difficult.

TREATING FOOD PROBLEMS

It is possible to handle food allergies and food intolerance yourself. Put your dog on a diet that it has never had. Obviously, if he has never eaten this new food, he can't have been allergic or intolerant of it. Start with a single ingredient that is not in the dog's diet at the present time. Ingredients like chopped beef or chicken are common in dogs' diets, so try something more exotic like rabbit, pheasant or another protein source. Keep the dog on this diet (with no additives) for a month. If the symptoms of food allergy or intolerance disappear, chances

are your dog has a food allergy.

Don't think that the single ingredient cured the problem. You still must find a suitable diet and ascertain which ingredient in the old diet was objectionable. This is most easily done by adding ingredients to the new diet one at a time. Let the dog stay on the modified diet for a month before you add another ingredient. Eventually, you will determine the ingredient that caused the adverse reaction.

An alternative method is to carefully study the ingredients in the diet to which your dog is allergic or intolerant. Identify the main ingredient in this diet and eliminate the main ingredient by buying a different food that does not have that ingredient. Keep experimenting until the symptoms disappear after one month on the new diet.

You should always have a canine first aid kit available to treat your dog for minor injuries. It is essential to be prepared for every possible mishap.

A male dog flea, *Ctenocephalides canis.*

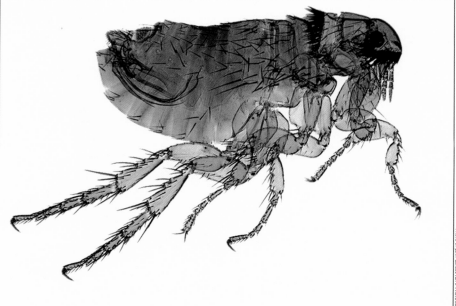

EXTERNAL PARASITES

FLEAS

Of all the problems to which dogs are prone, none is more well known and frustrating than fleas. Flea infestation is relatively simple to cure but difficult to prevent. Parasites that are harbored inside the body are a bit more difficult to eradicate but they are easier to control.

To control flea infestation, you have to understand the flea's life cycle. Fleas are often thought of as a summertime problem, but centrally heated homes have changed the patterns and fleas can be found at any time of the year. The most effective method of flea control is a two-stage approach: one stage to kill the adult fleas, and the other to control the development of pre-adult fleas. Unfortunately, no single active ingredient is effective against all stages of the life cycle.

FLEA KILLER CAUTION—"POISON"

Flea-killers are poisonous. You should not spray these toxic chemicals on areas of a dog's body that he licks, including his genitals and his face. Flea killers taken internally are a better answer, but check with your vet in case internal therapy is not advised for your dog.

LIFE CYCLE STAGES

During its life, a flea will pass through four life stages: egg, larva, pupa or nymph and adult. The adult stage is the most visible and irritating stage of the flea life cycle, and this is why the majority of flea-control products concentrate on this stage. The fact is that adult fleas account for only 1% of the total flea population, and the other 99% exist in pre-adult stages, i.e., eggs, larvae and nymphs. The pre-adult stages are barely visible to the naked eye.

THE LIFE CYCLE OF THE FLEA

Eggs are laid on the dog, usually in quantities of about 20 or 30, several times a day. The adult female flea must have a blood meal before each egg-laying session. When first laid, the eggs will cling to the dog's hair, as the eggs are still moist. However, they will quickly dry out and fall from the dog, especially if the dog moves around or scratches. Many eggs will fall off in the dog's favorite area or an area in which he spends a lot of time, such as his bed.

Once the eggs fall from the dog onto the carpet or furniture, they will hatch into larvae. This takes from one to ten days. Larvae are not particularly mobile and will usually travel only a few inches from where they hatch. However, they do have a tendency to move away from bright light and heavy

EN GARDE:
CATCHING FLEAS OFF GUARD!
Consider the following ways to arm yourself against fleas:
- Add a small amount of pennyroyal or eucalyptus oil to your dog's bath. These natural remedies repel fleas.
- Supplement your dog's food with fresh garlic (minced or grated) and a hearty amount of brewer's yeast, both of which ward off fleas.
- Use a flea comb on your dog daily. Submerge fleas in a cup of bleach to kill them quickly.
- Confine the dog to only a few rooms to limit the spread of fleas in the home.
- Vacuum daily...and get all of the crevices! Dispose of the bag every few days until the problem is under control.
- Wash your dog's bedding daily. Cover cushions where your dog sleeps with towels, and wash the towels often.

traffic—under furniture and behind doors are common places to find high quantities of flea larvae.

The flea larvae feed on dead organic matter, including adult flea feces, until they are ready to change into adult fleas. Fleas will usually remain as larvae for around seven days. After this period, the larvae will pupate into protective pupae. While inside the pupae, the larvae will undergo metamorphosis and change into adult fleas. This can take as little time as a few days, but the adult fleas can remain inside the pupae waiting to hatch for up to two years. The pupae are signaled to hatch by certain stimuli, such as physical pressure—the pupae's being stepped on, heat from an animal's lying on the pupae or increased carbon-dioxide levels and vibrations—indicating that a suitable host is available.

Once hatched, the adult flea must feed within a few days. Once the adult flea finds a host, it will not leave voluntarily. It only becomes dislodged by grooming or the host animal's scratching.

The adult flea will remain on the host for the duration of its life unless forcibly removed.

TREATING THE ENVIRONMENT AND THE DOG

Treating fleas should be a two-pronged attack. First, the environment needs to be treated; this includes carpets and furniture, especially the dog's bedding and areas underneath furniture. The environment should be treated with a household spray containing an Insect Growth Regulator (IGR) and an insecticide to kill the adult fleas. Most IGRs are effective against eggs and larvae; they actually mimic the fleas' own hormones and stop the eggs and larvae from developing into adult fleas. There are currently no treatments available to attack the pupa stage of the life cycle, so the adult insecticide is used to kill the newly hatched adult fleas before they find a host. Most IGRs are active for many months, while

A scanning electron micrograph of a dog or cat flea, *Ctenocephalides*, magnified more than 100x. This image has been colorized for effect.

THE LIFE CYCLE OF THE FLEA

Adult

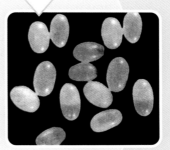

Egg

Larva

**Pupa
or
Nymph**

Fleas have been around for millions of years and have adapted to changing host animals. They are able to go through a complete life cycle in less than one month or they can extend their lives to almost two years by remaining as pupae or cocoons. They do not need blood or any other food for up to 20 months.

INSECT GROWTH REGULATOR (IGR)

Two types of products should be used when treating fleas—a product to treat the pet and a product to treat the home. Adult fleas represent less than 1% of the flea population. The pre-adult fleas (eggs, larvae and pupae) represent more than 99% of the flea population and are found in the environment; it is in the case of pre-adult fleas that products containing an Insect Growth Regulator (IGR) should be used in the home.

IGRs are a new class of compounds used to prevent the development of insects. They do not kill the insect outright, but instead use the insect's biology against it to stop it from completing its growth. Products that contain methoprene are the world's first and leading IGRs. Used to control fleas and other insects, this type of IGR will stop flea larvae from developing and protect the house for up to seven months.

The American dog tick, *Dermacentor variabilis*, is probably the most common tick found on dogs. Look at the strength in its eight legs! No wonder it's hard to detach them.

adult insecticides are only active for a few days.

When treating with a household spray, it is a good idea to vacuum before applying the product. This stimulates as many pupae as possible to hatch into adult fleas. The vacuum cleaner should also be treated with an insecticide to prevent the eggs and larvae that have been collected in the vacuum bag from hatching.

The second stage of treatment is to apply an adult insecticide to the dog. Traditionally, this would be in the form of a collar or a spray, but more recent innovations include digestible insecticides that poison the fleas when they ingest the dog's blood. Alternatively, there are drops that, when placed on the back of the dog's neck, spread throughout the hair and skin to kill adult fleas.

TICKS

Though not as common as fleas, ticks are found all over the tropical and temperate world. They don't bite, like fleas; they harpoon. They dig their sharp proboscis (nose) into the dog's skin and drink the blood. Their

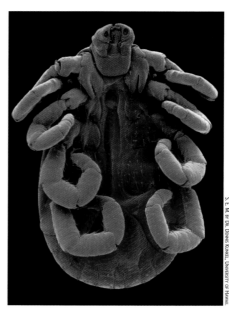

S. E. M. BY DR. DENNIS KUNKEL, UNIVERSITY OF HAWAII.

only food and drink is dog's blood. Dogs can get Lyme disease, Rocky Mountain spotted fever, tick bite paralysis and many other diseases from ticks. They may live where fleas are found and they like to hide in cracks or seams in walls. They are controlled the same way fleas are controlled.

The American dog tick, *Dermacentor variabilis*, may well be the most common dog tick in many geographical areas, especially those areas where the climate is hot and humid. Most dog ticks have life expectancies of a week to six months, depending upon climatic conditions. They can neither jump nor fly, but they can crawl slowly and can range up to 16 feet to reach a sleeping or unsuspecting dog.

MITES

Just as fleas and ticks can be problematic for your dog, mites can also lead to an itchy nuisance. Microscopic in size, mites are related to ticks and generally take up permanent residence on their host animal—in this case, your dog! The term *mange* refers to any infestation caused by one of the mighty mites, of which there are six varieties that concern dog owners.

Demodex mites cause a condition known as demodicosis

DEER-TICK CROSSING
The great outdoors may be fun for your dog, but it also is a home to dangerous ticks. Deer ticks carry a bacterium known as *Borrelia burgdorferi* and are most active in the autumn and spring. When infections are caught early, penicillin and tetracycline are effective antibiotics, but, if left untreated, the bacteria may cause neurological, kidney and cardiac problems as well as long-term trouble with walking and painful joints.

S.E.M. BY DR. ANDREW SPIELMAN/PHOTOTAKE

PHOTO BY DR. DENNIS KUNKEL, UNIVERSITY OF HAWAII

The head of an American dog tick, *Dermacentor variabilis*, enlarged and colorized for effect.

Photo by James Hayden/Yoav/Phototake.

Human lice look like dog lice; the two are closely related.

Photo by Dwight R. Kuhn.

(sometimes called red mange or follicular mange), in which the mites live in the dog's hair follicles and sebaceous glands in larger-than-normal numbers. This type of mange is commonly passed from the dam to her puppies and usually shows up on the puppies' muzzles, though demodicosis is not transferable from one normal dog to another. Most dogs recover from this type of mange without any treatment, though topical therapies are commonly prescribed by the vet.

The *Cheyletiellosis* mite is the hook-mouthed culprit associated with "walking dandruff," a condition that affects dogs as well as cats and rabbits. This mite lives on the surface of the animal's skin and is readily transferable through direct or indirect contact with an affected animal. The dandruff is present in the form of scaly skin, which may or may not be itchy. If not treated, this mange can affect a whole kennel of dogs and can be spread to humans as well.

The *Sarcoptes* mite causes intense itching on the dog in the form of a condition known as scabies or sarcoptic mange. The cycle of the *Sarcoptes* mite lasts about three weeks, and the mites live in the top layer of the dog's skin (epidermis), preferably in areas with little hair. Scabies is highly contagious and can be passed to humans. Sometimes an allergic reaction to the mite worsens the severe itching associated with sarcoptic mange.

Ear mites, *Otodectes cynotis,* lead to otodectic mange, which most commonly affects the outer ear canal of the dog, though other areas can be affected as well. Dogs with ear-mite infestation commonly scratch at their ears, causing further irritation, and shake their heads. Dark brown droppings in the outer ear confirm the diagnosis. Your vet can prescribe a treatment to flush out the ears and kill any eggs in the ears. A complete month of treatment is necessary to cure the mange.

Two other mites, less common in dogs, include *Dermanyssus gallinae* (the poultry or red mite) and *Eutrombicula alfreddugesi* (the North American mite associated with trombiculidiasis or chigger infestation). The poultry mite frequently lives on chickens, but can transfer to dogs who spend time near farm animals. Chigger infestation affects dogs in the

DO NOT MIX
Never mix parasite-control products without first consulting your vet. Some products can become toxic when combined with others and can cause fatal consequences.

NOT A DROP TO DRINK
Never allow your dog to swim in polluted water or public areas where water quality can be suspect. Even perfectly clear water can harbor parasites, many of which can cause serious to fatal illnesses in canines. Areas inhabited by waterfowl and other wildlife are especially dangerous.

Central US who have exposure to woodlands. The types of mange caused by both of these mites are treatable by vets.

INTERNAL PARASITES
Most animals—fishes, birds and mammals, including dogs and humans—have worms and other parasites that live inside their bodies. According to Dr. Herbert R. Axelrod, the fish pathologist, there are two kinds of parasites: dumb and smart. The smart parasites live in peaceful cooperation with their hosts (symbiosis), while the dumb parasites kill their hosts. Most worm infections are relatively easy to control. If they are not controlled, they weaken the host dog to the point that other medical problems occur, but they do not kill the host as dumb parasites would.

A brown dog tick, *Rhipicephalus sanguineus*, is an uncommon but annoying tick found on dogs.
PHOTO BY CAROLINA BIOLOGICAL SUPPLY/PHOTOTAKE.

The roundworm *Rhabditis* can infect both dogs and humans.

ROUNDWORMS

Average-size dogs can pass 1,360,000 roundworm eggs every day. For example, if there were only 1 million dogs in the world, the world would be saturated with thousands of tons of dog feces. These feces would contain around 15,000,000,000 roundworm eggs.

Up to 31% of home yards and children's sand boxes in the US contain roundworm eggs.

Flushing dog's feces down the toilet is not a safe practice because the usual sewage treatments do not destroy roundworm eggs.

Infected puppies start shedding roundworm eggs at three weeks of age. They can be infected by their mother's milk.

The roundworm, *Ascaris lumbricoides.*

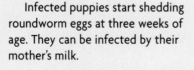

ROUNDWORMS

The roundworms that infect dogs are known scientifically as *Toxocara canis.* They live in the dog's intestines and shed eggs continually. It has been estimated that a dog produces about 6 or more ounces of feces every day. Each ounce of feces averages hundreds of thousands of roundworm eggs. There are no known areas in which dogs roam that do not contain roundworm eggs. The greatest danger of roundworms is that they infect people, too! It is wise to have your dog tested regularly for roundworms.

In young puppies, roundworms cause bloated bellies, diarrhea, coughing and vomiting, and are transmitted from the dam (through blood or milk). Affected puppies will not appear as animated as normal puppies. The worms appear spaghetti-like, measuring as long as 6 inches. Adult dogs can acquire roundworms through coprophagia (eating contaminated feces) or by killing rodents that carry roundworms.

Roundworm infection can kill puppies and cause severe problems in adults, as the hatched larvae travel to the lungs and trachea through the bloodstream. Cleanliness is the best preventative for roundworms. Always pick up after your dog and dispose of feces in appropriate receptacles.

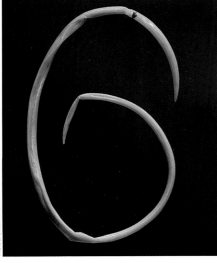

PHOTO BY DWIGHT R. KUHN.

HOOKWORMS

In the United States, dog owners have to be concerned about four different species of hookworm, the most common and most serious of which is *Ancylostoma caninum,* which prefers warm climates. The others are *Ancylostoma braziliense, Ancylostoma tubaeforme* and *Uncinaria stenocephala,* the latter of which is a concern to dogs living in the Northern US and Canada, as this species prefers cold climates. Hookworms are dangerous to humans as well as to dogs and cats, and can be the cause of severe anemia due to iron deficiency. The worm uses its teeth to attach itself to the dog's intestines and changes the site of its attachment about six times per day. Each time the worm

repositions itself, the dog loses blood and can become anemic. *Ancylostoma caninum* is the most likely of the four species to cause anemia in the dog.

Symptoms of hookworm infection include dark stools, weight loss, general weakness, pale coloration and anemia, as well as possible skin problems. Fortunately, hookworms are easily purged from the affected dog with a number of medications that have proven effective. Discuss these with your vet. Most heartworm preventatives include a hookworm insecticide as well.

Owners also must be aware that hookworms can infect humans, who can acquire the larvae through exposure to contaminated feces. Since the worms cannot complete their life cycle on a human, the worms simply infest the skin and cause irritation. This condition is known as cutaneous larva migrans syndrome. As a preventative, use disposable gloves or a "poop-scoop" to pick up your dog's droppings and prevent your dog (or neighborhood cats) from defecating in children's play areas.

The hookworm, *Ancylostoma caninum.*

PHOTO BY C. JAMES WEBB/PHOTOTAKE.

The infective stage of the hookworm larva.

TAPEWORMS

Humans, rats, squirrels, foxes, coyotes, wolves and domestic dogs are all susceptible to tapeworm infection. Except in humans, tapeworms are usually not a fatal infection. Infected individuals can harbor 1000 parasitic worms.

Tapeworms, like some other types of worm, are hermaphroditic, meaning male and female in the same worm.

If dogs eat infected rats or mice, or anything else infected with tapeworm, they get the tapeworm disease. One month after attaching to a dog's intestine, the worm starts shedding eggs. These eggs are infective immediately. Infective eggs can live for a few months without a host animal.

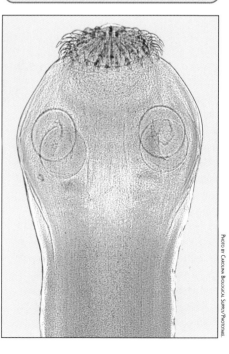

The head and rostellum (the round prominence on the scolex) of a tapeworm, which infects dogs and humans.

PHOTO BY CAROLINA BIOLOGICAL SUPPLY/PHOTOTAKE.

TAPEWORMS

There are many species of tapeworm, all of which are carried by fleas! The most common tapeworm affecting dogs is known as *Dipylidium caninum*. The dog eats the flea and starts the tapeworm cycle. Humans can also be infected with tapeworms—so don't eat fleas! Fleas are so small that your dog could pass them onto your hands, your plate or your food and thus make it possible for you to ingest a flea that is carrying tapeworm eggs.

While tapeworm infection is not life-threatening in dogs (smart parasite!), it can be the cause of a very serious liver disease for humans. About 50% of the humans infected with *Echinococcus multilocularis*, a type of tapeworm that causes alveolar hydatid, perish.

WHIPWORMS

In North America, whipworms are counted among the most common parasitic worms in dogs. The whipworm's scientific name is *Trichuris vulpis*. These worms attach themselves in the lower parts of the intestine, where they feed. Affected dogs may only experience upset tummies, colic and diarrhea. These worms, however, can live for months or years in the dog, beginning their larval stage in the small intestine, spending their adult stage in the large intestine and finally passing infective eggs through the dog's feces. The only way to detect whipworms is through a fecal examination, though this is not always foolproof. Treatment for whipworms is tricky, due to the worms' unusual life-cycle pattern, and very often dogs are reinfected due to exposure to infective eggs on the ground. The whipworm eggs can survive in the environment for as long as five years; thus, cleaning up droppings in your own backyard as well as in public places is absolutely essential for sanitation purposes and the health of your dog and others.

THREADWORMS

Though less common than roundworms, hookworms and those previously mentioned, threadworms concern dog owners in the Southwestern US and Gulf Coast area where the climate is hot and humid. Living in the small intestine of the dog, this worm measures a mere 2 millimeters and is round in shape. Like that of the whipworm, the threadworm's life cycle is very complex and the eggs and larvae are passed through the feces. A deadly disease in humans, *Strongyloides* readily infects people, and the handling of feces is the most common means of transmission. Threadworms are most often seen in young puppies; bloody diarrhea and pneumonia are symptoms. Sick puppies must be isolated and treated immediately; vets recommend a follow-up treatment one month later.

HEARTWORM PREVENTATIVES

There are many heartworm preventatives on the market, many of which are sold at your veterinarian's office. These products can be given daily or monthly, depending on the manufacturer's instructions. All of these preventatives contain chemical insecticides directed at killing heartworms, which leads to some controversy among dog owners. In effect, heartworm preventatives are necessary evils, though you should determine how necessary based on your pet's lifestyle. There is no doubt that heartworm is a dreadful disease that threatens the lives of dogs. However, the likelihood of your dog's being bitten by an infected mosquito is slim in most places, and a mosquito-repellent (or an herbal remedy such as Wormwood or Black Walnut) is much safer for your dog and will not compromise his immune system (the way heartworm preventatives will). Should you decide to use the traditional preventative "medications," you can consider giving the pill every other or third month. Since the toxins in the pill will kill the heartworms at all stages of development, the pill would be effective in killing larvae, nymphs or adults, and it takes four months for the larvae to reach the adult stage. Thus, there is no rationale to poisoning the dog's system on a monthly basis. Lastly, do not give the pill during the winter months since there are no mosquitoes around to pass on their infection, unless you live in a tropical environment.

Life Cycle of the Heartworm

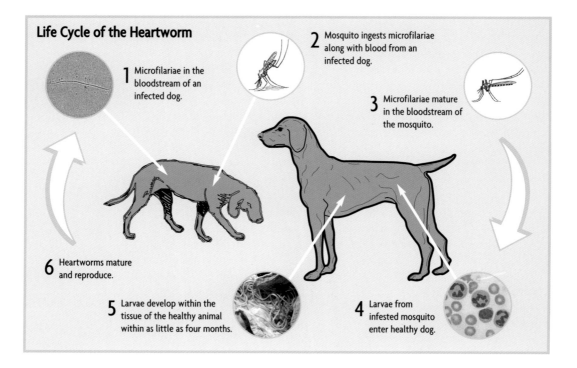

1 Microfilariae in the bloodstream of an infected dog.

2 Mosquito ingests microfilariae along with blood from an infected dog.

3 Microfilariae mature in the bloodstream of the mosquito.

4 Larvae from infested mosquito enter healthy dog.

5 Larvae develop within the tissue of the healthy animal within as little as four months.

6 Heartworms mature and reproduce.

HEARTWORMS

Heartworms are thin, extended worms up to 12 inches long, which live in a dog's heart and the major blood vessels surrounding it. Dogs may have up to 200 worms. Symptoms may be loss of energy, loss of appetite, coughing, the development of a pot belly and anemia.

Heartworms are transmitted by mosquitoes. The mosquito drinks the blood of an infected dog and takes in larvae with the blood. The larvae, called microfilariae, develop within the body of the mosquito and are passed on to the next dog bitten after the larvae mature. It takes two to three weeks for the larvae to develop to the infective stage within the body of the mosquito. Dogs are usually treated at about six weeks of age and maintained on a prophylactic dose given monthly.

Blood testing for heartworms is not necessarily indicative of how seriously your dog is infected. Although this is a dangerous disease, it is not easy for a dog to be infected. Discuss the various preventatives with your vet, as there are many different types now available. Together you can decide on a safe course of prevention for your dog.

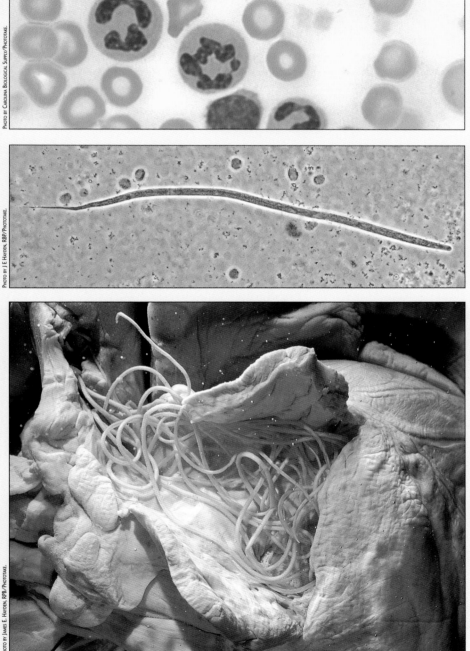

Magnified
heartworm larvae,
Dirofilaria immitis.

Heartworm,
*Dirofilaria
immitis.*

The heart
of a dog infected
with canine
heartworm,
*Dirofilaria
immitis.*

HOMEOPATHY:
an alternative to conventional medicine

"Less is Most"

Using this principle, the strength of a homeopathic remedy is measured by the number of serial dilutions that were undertaken to create it. The greater the number of serial dilutions, the greater the strength of the homeopathic remedy. The potency of a remedy that has been made by making a dilution of 1 part in 100 parts (or 1/100) is 1c or 1cH. If this remedy is subjected to a series of further dilutions, each one being 1/100, a more dilute and stronger remedy is produced. If the remedy is diluted in this way six times, it is called 6c or 6cH. A dilution of 6c is 1 part in 1000,000,000,000. In general, higher potencies in more frequent doses are better for acute symptoms and lower potencies in more infrequent doses are more useful for chronic, long-standing problems.

CURING OUR DOGS NATURALLY
Holistic medicine means treating the whole animal as a unique, perfect living being. Generally, holistic treatments do not suppress the symptoms that the body naturally produces, as do most medications prescribed by conventional doctors and vets. Holistic methods seek to cure disease by regaining balance and harmony in the patient's environment. Some of these methods include use of nutritional therapy, herbs, flower essences, aromatherapy, acupuncture, massage, chiropractic and, of course, the most popular holistic approach, homeopathy.

Homeopathy is a theory or system of treating illness with small doses of substances which, if administered in larger quantities, would produce the symptoms that the patient already has. This approach is often described as "like cures like." Although modern veterinary medicine is geared toward the "quick fix," homeopathy relies on the belief that, given the time, the body is able to heal itself and return to its natural, healthy state.

Choosing a remedy to cure a problem in our dogs is the difficult part of homeopathy. Consult with your veterinarian for a professional diagnosis of your dog's symptoms. Often these symptoms require immediate conventional care. If your vet is willing and knowledgeable, you may attempt a homeopathic remedy. Be aware that cortisone prevents homeopathic remedies from working. There are hundreds of possibilities and combinations to cure many problems in dogs, from basic physical problems such as excessive shedding, fleas or other parasites, unattractive doggy odor, bad breath, upset stomach, obesity, dry, oily or dull coat, diarrhea, ear problems or eye discharge (including tears and dry or mucusy matter), to behavioral abnormalities such as fear of loud noises, habitual licking, poor appetite, excessive barking and various phobias. From alumina to zincum metallicum, the remedies span the planet and the imagination…from flowers and weeds to chemicals, insect droppings, diesel smoke and volcanic ash.

Using "Like to Treat Like"

Unlike conventional medicines that suppress symptoms, homeopathic remedies treat illnesses with small doses of substances that, if administered in larger quantities, would produce the symptoms that the patient already has. While the same homeopathic remedy can be used to treat different symptoms in different dogs, here are some interesting remedies and their uses.

Apis Mellifica
(made from honey bee venom) can be used for allergies or to reduce swelling that occurs in acutely infected kidneys.

Diesel Smoke
can be used to help control motion sickness.

Calcarea Fluorica
(made from calcium fluoride, which helps harden bone structure) can be useful in treating hard lumps in tissues.

Natrum Muriaticum
(made from common salt, sodium chloride) is useful in treating thin, thirsty dogs.

Nitricum Acidum
(made from nitric acid) is used for symptoms you would expect to see from contact with acids such as lesions, especially where the skin joins the linings of body orifices or openings such as the lips and nostrils.

Symphytum
(made from the herb Knitbone, *Symphytum officianale*) is used to encourage bones to heal.

Urtica Urens
(made from the common stinging nettle) is used in treating painful, irritating rashes.

First Aid at a Glance

Burns
Place the affected area under cool water; use ice if only a small area is burnt.

Bee stings/Insect bites
Apply ice to relieve swelling; antihistamine dosed properly.

Animal bites
Clean any bleeding area; apply pressure until bleeding subsides; go to the vet.

Spider bites
Use cold compress and a pressurized pack to inhibit venom's spreading.

Antifreeze poisoning
Induce vomiting with hydrogen peroxide. Seek *immediate* veterinary help!

Fish hooks
Removal best handled by vet; hook must be cut in order to remove.

Snake bites
Pack ice around bite; contact vet quickly; identify snake for proper antivenin.

Car accident
Move dog from roadway with blanket; seek veterinary aid.

Shock
Calm the dog; keep him warm; seek immediate veterinary help.

Nosebleed
Apply cold compress to the nose; apply pressure to any visible abrasion.

Bleeding
Apply pressure above the area; treat wound by applying a cotton pack.

Heat stroke
Submerge dog in cold bath; cool down with fresh air and water; go to the vet.

Frostbite/Hypothermia
Warm the dog with a warm bath, electric blankets or hot water bottles.

Abrasions
Clean the wound and wash out thoroughly with fresh water; apply antiseptic.

Remember: an injured dog may attempt to bite a helping hand from fear and confusion. Always muzzle the dog before trying to offer assistance.

Recognizing a Sick Dog

Unlike colicky babies and cranky children, our canine kids cannot tell us when they are feeling ill. Therefore, there are a number of signs that owners can identify to know that their dogs are not feeling well.

Take note for physical manifestations such as:

- unusual, bad odor, including bad breath
- excessive shedding
- wax in the ears, chronic ear irritation
- oily, flaky, dull haircoat
- mucus, tearing or similar discharge in the eyes
- fleas or mites
- mucus in stool, diarrhea
- sensitivity to petting or handling
- licking at paws, scratching face, etc.

Keep an eye out for behavioral changes as well including:

- lethargy, idleness
- lack of patience or general irritability
- lack of interest in food
- phobias (fear of people, loud noises, etc.)
- strange behavior, suspicion, fear
- coprophagia
- more frequent barking
- whimpering, crying

Get Well Soon

You don't need a DVM to provide good TLC to your sick or recovering dog, but you do need to pay attention to some details that normally wouldn't bother him. The following tips will aid Fido's recovery and get him back on his paws again:

- Keep his space free of irritating smells, like heavy perfumes and air fresheners.
- Rest is the best medicine! Avoid harsh lighting that will prevent your dog from sleeping. Shade him from bright sunlight during the day and dim the lights in the evening.
- Keep the noise level down. Animals are more sensitive to sound when they are sick.

- Be attentive to any necessary temperature adjustments. A dog with a fever needs a cool room and cold liquids. A bitch that is whelping or recovering from surgery will be more comfortable in a warm room, consuming warm liquids and food.
- You wouldn't send a sick child back to school early, so don't rush your dog back into a full routine until he seems absolutely ready.

Owners and breeders always strive for Pugs with clear, healthy eyes.

A PET OWNER'S GUIDE TO COMMON OPHTHALMIC DISEASES
by Prof. Dr. Robert L. Peiffer, Jr.

Few would argue that vision is the most important of the cognitive senses, and maintenance of a normal visual system is important for an optimal quality of life. Likewise, pet owners tend to be acutely aware of their pet's eyes and vision, which is important because early detection of ocular disease will optimize therapeutic outcomes. The eye is a sensitive organ with minimal reparative capabilities, and with some diseases, such as glaucoma, uveitis and retinal detachment, diagnosis and treatment can be critical in terms of whether vision can be preserved.

Lower entropion, or rolling in of the eyelid, is causing irritation in the left eye of this young dog. Several extra eye lashes, or distichiasis, are present on the upper lid.

The causes of ocular disease are quite varied; the nature of dogs makes them susceptible to traumatic conditions, the most common of which include proptosis of the globe, cat scratch injuries and penetrating wounds from foreign objects, including sticks and BB-gun pellets. Infectious diseases caused by bacteria, viruses or fungi may be localized to the eye or part of a systemic infection. Many of the common conditions, including eyelid conformational problems, cataracts, glaucoma and retinal degenerations, have a genetic basis.

Before acquiring your puppy, it is important to ascertain that both parents have been examined and certified free of eye disease by a veterinary ophthalmologist. Since many of these genetic diseases can be detected early in life, acquire the pup with the condition that it pass a thorough ophthalmic examination by a qualified specialist.

LID CONFORMATIONAL ABNORMALITIES
Rolling in (entropion) or out (ectropion) of the lids tends to be a breed-related problem. Entropion can involve the upper and/or lower lids. Signs usually appear between 3 and 12 months of age. The irritation caused by the eyelid hairs' rubbing

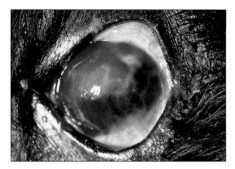

on the surface of the cornea may result in blinking, tearing and damage to the cornea. Ectropion is likewise breed-related and is considered "normal" in hounds, for instance. Unlike entropion, which results in acute discomfort, ectropion may cause chronic irritation related to exposure and the pooling of secretions. Most of these cases can be managed medically with daily irrigation with sterile saline and topical antibiotics when required.

EYELASH ABNORMALITIES
Dogs normally have lashes only on the upper lids, in contrast to humans. Occasionally, extra eyelashes may be seen emerging at the eyelid margin (distichiasis) or through the inner surface of the eyelid (ectopic cilia).

CONJUNCTIVITIS
Inflammation of the conjunctiva, the pink tissue that lines the lids and the anterior portion of the sclera, is generally accompanied by redness, discharge and mild discomfort. The majority of cases are associated either with bacterial infections or with dry eye syndrome. Fortunately, topical medications are generally effective in curing or controlling the problem.

DRY EYE SYNDROME
Dry eye syndrome (keratoconjunctivitis sicca) is a common cause of external ocular disease. Discharge is typically thick and sticky, and keratitis is a frequent component; any breed can be affected. While some cases can be associated with the toxic effects of drugs, including the sulfa antibiotics, the cause in the majority of the cases cannot be determined and is assumed to be immune-mediated.

Keratoconjunctivitis sicca, seen here in the right eye of a middle-aged dog, causes a characteristic thick mucus discharge as well as secondary corneal changes.

Left: Prolapse of the gland of the third eyelid in the right eye of a pup. Right: In this case, in the right eye of a young dog, the prolapsed gland can be seen emerging between the edge of the third eyelid and the corneal surface.

Multiple deep ulcerations affect the cornea of this middle-aged dog.

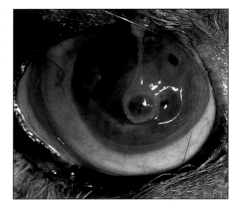

PROLAPSE OF THE GLAND OF THE THIRD EYELID

In this condition, commonly referred to as *cherry eye*, the gland of the third eyelid, which produces about one-third of the aqueous phase of the tear film and is normally situated within the anterior orbit, prolapses to emerge as a pink fleshy mass protruding over the edge of the third eyelid, between the third eyelid and the cornea. The condition usually develops during the first year of life and, while mild irritation may result, the condition is unsightly as much as anything else.

Lipid deposition can occur as a primary inherited dystrophy, or secondarily to hypercholesterolemia (in dogs frequently associated with hypothyroidism), chronic corneal inflammation or neoplasia. The deposits in this dog assume an oval pattern in the center of the cornea.

CORNEAL DISEASE

The cornea is the clear front part of the eye that provides the first step in the collection of light on its journey eventually to be focused onto the retina, and most corneal diseases will be manifested by alterations in corneal transparency. The cornea is an exquisitely innervated tissue, and defects in corneal integrity are accompanied by pain, which is demonstrated by squinting.

Corneal ulcers may occur secondary to trauma or to irritation from entropion or ectopic cilia. In middle-aged or older dogs, epithelial ulcerations may occur spontaneously due to an inherent defect; these are referred to as indolent or Boxer ulcers, in recognition of the breed in which we see the condition most frequently. Infection may occur secondarily. Ulcers can be potentially blinding conditions; severity is dependent upon the size and depth of the ulcer and other complicating features.

Non-ulcerative keratitis tends to have an immune-mediated component and is managed by topical immunosuppressants, usually corticosteroids. Corneal edema can occur in elderly dogs. It is due to a failure of the corneal endothelial "pump."

The cornea responds to chronic irritation by transforming

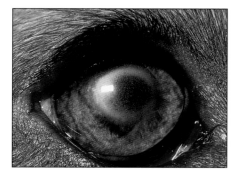

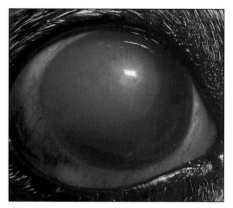

into skin-like tissue that is evident clinically by pigmentation, scarring and vascularization; some cases may respond to tear stimulants, lubricants and topical corticosteroids, while others benefit from surgical narrowing of the eyelid opening in order to enhance corneal protection.

UVEITIS

Inflammation of the vascular tissue of the eye—the uvea—is a common and potentially serious disease in dogs. While it may occur secondarily to trauma or other intraocular diseases, such as

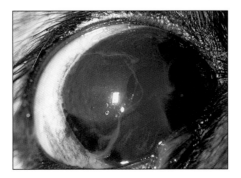

cataracts, most commonly uveitis is associated with some type of systemic infectious or neoplastic process. Uncontrolled, uveitis can lead to blinding cataracts, glaucoma and/or retinal detachments, and aggressive symptomatic therapy with dilating agents (to prevent pupillary adhesions) and anti-inflammatories are critical.

GLAUCOMA

The eye is essentially a hollow fluid-filled sphere, and the pressure within is maintained by regulation of the rate of fluid production and fluid egress at 10–20 mms of mercury. The retinal cells are extremely sensitive to elevations of intraocular pressure and, unless controlled, permanent blindness can occur within hours to days. In acute glaucoma, the conjunctiva becomes congested, the cornea cloudy, the pupil moderate and fixed; the eye is generally painful and avisual. Increased constant signs of

Corneal edema can develop as a slowly progressive process in elderly Boston Terriers, Miniature Dachshunds and Miniature Poodles, as well as others, as a result of the inability of the corneal endothelial "pump" to maintain a state of dehydration.

Medial pigmentary keratitis in this dog is associated with irritation from prominent facial folds.

Glaucoma in the dog most commonly occurs as a sudden extreme elevation of intraocular pressure, frequently to three to four times the norm. The eye of this dog demonstrates the common signs of episcleral injection, or redness; mild diffuse corneal cloudiness, due to edema; and a mid-sized fixed pupil.

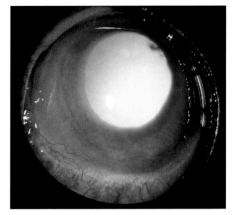

discomfort will accompany chronic cases.

Management of glaucoma is one of the most challenging situations that the veterinary ophthalmologist faces; in spite of intense efforts, many of these cases will result in blindness.

CATARACTS AND LENS DISLOCATION

Cataracts are the most common blinding condition in dogs; fortunately, they are readily amenable to surgical intervention, with excellent results in terms of restoration of vision and replace-

ment of the cataractous lens with a synthetic one. Most cataracts in dogs are inherited; less commonly cataracts can be secondary to trauma; to other ocular diseases, including uveitis, glaucoma, lens luxation and retinal degeneration; or secondary to an underlying systemic metabolic disease, including diabetes and Cushing's disease. Signs include a progressive loss of the bright dark appearance of the pupil, which is replaced by a blue-gray hazy appearance. In this respect, cataracts need to be distinguished from the normal aging process of nuclear sclerosis, which occurs in middle-aged or older animals, and has minimal effect on vision.

Lens dislocation occurs in dogs and frequently leads to secondary glaucoma; early removal of the dislocated lens is generally curative.

RETINAL DISEASE

Retinal degenerations are usually inherited, but may be associated with vitamin E deficiency in dogs.

Left: The typical posterior subcapsular cataract appears between one and two years of age, but rarely progresses to where the animal has visual problems. Right: Inherited cataracts generally appear between three and six years of age, and progress to the stage seen where functional vision is significantly impaired.

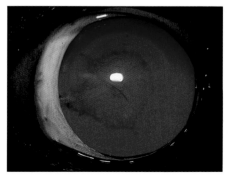

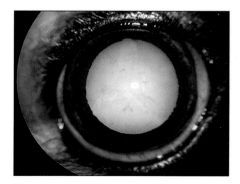

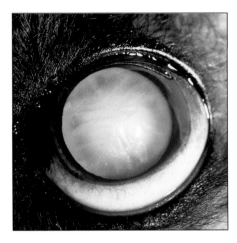

While signs are variable, most frequently one notes a decrease in vision over a period of months, which typically starts out as night blindness. The cause of a more rapid loss of vision due to retinal degeneration that occurs over days to weeks is labeled sudden acquired retinal degeneration or SARD; the outcome, however, is unfortunately usually similar to inherited and nutritional conditions, as the retinal tissues possess minimal regenerative capabilities. Most pets, however, with a bit of extra care and attention, show an amazing ability to adapt to an avisual world, and can be maintained as pets with a satisfactory quality of life.

Detachment of the retina—due to accumulation of blood between the retina and the underling uvea, which is called the *choroid*—can occur secondarily to retinal tears or holes, tractional forces within the eye, or as a result of uveitis. These types of detachments may be amenable to surgical repair if diagnosed early.

OPTIC NEURITIS
Optic neuritis, or inflammation of the nerve that connects the eye with the brain stem, is a relatively uncommon condition that presents usually with rather sudden loss of vision and widely dilated non-responsive pupils.

Anterior lens luxation can occur as a primary disease in the terrier breeds, or secondarily to trauma. The fibers that hold the lens in place rupture and the lens may migrate through the pupil to be situated in front of the iris. Secondary glaucoma is a frequent and significant compli-cation that can be avoided if the dislocated lens is removed surgically.

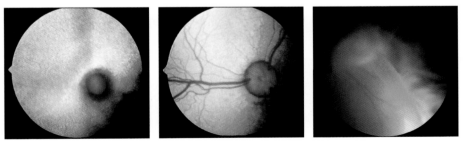

Left: The posterior pole of a normal fundus is shown; prominent are the head of the optic nerve and the retinal blood vessels. The retina is transparent, and the prominent green tapetum is seen superiorly.
Center: An eye with inherited retinal dysplasia is depicted. The tapetal retina superior to the optic disc is disorganized, with multifocal areas of hyperplasia of the retinal pigment epithelium.
Right: Severe collie eye anomaly and a retinal detachment; this eye is unfortunately blind.

If you have a
well-bred and
properly trained
Pug, you may
wish to pursue
the exciting sport
of showing dogs.

SHOWING YOUR

PUG

When you purchase your Pug, you will make it clear to the breeder whether you want one just as a loveable companion and pet, or if you hope to be buying a Pug with show prospects. No reputable breeder will sell you a young puppy and tell you that it is *definitely* of show quality, for so much can go wrong during the early months of a puppy's development. If you plan to show, what you hopefully will have acquired is a puppy with "show potential."

To the novice, exhibiting a Pug in the show ring may look easy, but it takes a lot of hard work and devotion to do top winning at a show such as the prestigious Westminster Kennel Club dog show, not to mention a little luck too!

The first concept that the canine novice learns when watching a dog show is that each dog first competes against members of his own breed. Once the judge has selected the best member of each breed (Best of Breed), provided that the show is judged on a Group system, that chosen dog will compete with other dogs in his group. Finally, the dogs chosen first in each group will compete for Best in Show.

The second concept that you must understand is that the dogs are not actually compared against one another. The judge compares each dog against his breed standard, the written description of the ideal specimen that is approved by the American Kennel Club (AKC). While some early breed standards indeed were based on specific dogs that were famous or popular, many dedicated enthusiasts say that a perfect specimen, as described in the standard, has never walked into a show ring, has never been bred and, to the woe of dog breeders around the globe, does not exist. Breeders attempt to get as close to this ideal as possible with every litter, but theoretically the "perfect" dog is so elusive that it is impossible. (And if the "perfect" dog were born, breeders and judges would probably never agree that it was indeed "perfect.")

If you are interested in

AKC GROUPS

For showing purposes, the American Kennel Club divides its recognized breeds into seven groups: Sporting Dogs, Hounds, Working Dogs, Terriers, Toys, Non-Sporting Dogs and Herding Dogs. The Pug is shown in the Toy Group.

exploring the world of dog showing, your best bet is to join your local breed club or the national or parent club, which is the Pug Dog Club of America. These clubs often host both regional and national specialties, shows for Pugs only, which can include conformation as well as obedience and other special events. Even if you have no intention of competing with your Pug, a specialty is like a festival for lovers of the breed who congregate to share their favorite topic: Pugs! Clubs also send out newsletters, and some organize training days and seminars in order that people may learn more about their chosen breed. To locate the breed club closest to you, contact the American Kennel Club, which furnishes the rules and regulations for all of these events plus general dog registration and other basic requirements of dog ownership.

The American Kennel Club offers three kinds of conformation shows; an all-breed show (for all AKC-recognized breeds), a specialty show (for one breed only, usually sponsored by the parent club) and a Group show (for all breeds in the Group).

For a dog to become an AKC champion of record, the dog must accumulate 15 points at the shows from at least three different judges, including two "majors." A "major" is defined as a three-, four- or five-point win, and the number of points per win is determined by

All show dogs are crate-trained! Top breeders travel to the show grounds with a van full of potential winners, all of whom are cozily tucked away in their crates until the competition begins.

the number of dogs entered in the show on that day. Depending on the breed, the number of points that are awarded varies. In a breed as popular as the Pug, more dogs are needed to rack up the points. At any dog show, only one dog and one bitch of each breed can win points.

Dog showing does not offer "co-ed" classes. Dogs and bitches never compete against each other in the classes. Non-champion dogs are called "class dogs" because they compete in one of five classes. A dog is entered in a particular class depending on age and previous show wins. To begin, there is the Puppy Class (for 6- to 9-month-olds and for 9- to 12-month-olds); this class is followed by the Novice Class (for dogs that have not won any first prizes except in the Puppy Class or three first prizes in the Novice Class and have not accumulated any points toward their champion title); the Bred-by-Exhibitor Class (for dogs handled by their breeders or handled by one of the breeder's immediate family); the American-bred Class; and the Open Class (for any dog that is not a champion).

The judge at the show begins judging the Puppy Class, first dogs and then bitches, and proceeds through the classes. The judge places his winners first through fourth in each class. In the Winners Class, the first-place winners of each class compete

MEET THE AKC
The AKC is the main governing body of the dog sport in the United States. Founded in 1884, the AKC consists of 500 or more independent dog clubs plus 4,500 affiliate clubs, all of which follow the AKC rules and regulations. Additionally, the AKC maintains a registry for pure-bred dogs in the US and works to preserve the integrity of the sport and its continuation in the country. Over 1,000,000 dogs are registered each year, representing about 150 recognized breeds.

with one another to determine Winners Dog and Winners Bitch. The judge also places a Reserve Winners Dog and Reserve Winners Bitch, which could be awarded the points in the case of a disqualification. The Winners Dog and Winners Bitch—the two that are awarded the points for the breed—then compete with any champions of record entered in the show. The judge reviews the Winners Dog, Winners Bitch and all of the champions to select his Best of Breed. The Best of Winners is selected between the Winners Dog and Winners Bitch. Were one of these two to be selected Best of Breed, he or she would automatically be named Best of Winners as well. Finally the judge selects his Best of Opposite Sex to the Best of Breed winner.

At a Group show or all-breed show, the Best of Breed winners from each breed then compete against one another for Group One through Group Four. The judge compares each Best of Breed to his breed standard, and the dog that most closely lives up to the ideal for his breed is selected as Group One. Finally, all seven group winners (from the Toy Group, Sporting Group, Hound Group, etc.) compete for Best in Show.

To find out about dog shows in your area, you can subscribe to the American Kennel Club's monthly magazine, the *American Kennel Gazette* and the accompanying *Events Calendar*. You can also look in your local newspaper for advertisements for dog shows in your area or go on the Internet to the AKC's website, www.akc.org.

If your Pug is six months of age or older and registered with the AKC, you can enter him in a dog show where the breed is offered classes. Provided that your Pug does not have a disqualifying fault, he can compete. Only unaltered dogs can be entered in a dog show, so if you have spayed or neutered your Pug, you cannot compete in conformation shows. The reason for this is simple. Dog shows are the main forum to prove which representatives of a breed are worthy of being bred. Only dogs that have achieved championships—the AKC "seal of approval" for quality in pure-bred dogs—should be bred. Altered dogs, however, can participate in other AKC events such as obedience trials and the Canine Good Citizen® program.

Before you actually step into the ring, you would be well advised to sit back and observe the

CLUB CONTACTS

You can get information about dog shows from the national kennel clubs:

American Kennel Club
5580 Centerview Dr., Raleigh, NC 27606-3390
www.akc.org

United Kennel Club
100 E. Kilgore Road, Kalamazoo, MI 49002
www.ukcdogs.com

Canadian Kennel Club
89 Skyway Ave., Suite 100, Etobicoke, Ontario
M9W 6R4 Canada
www.ckc.ca

The Kennel Club
1-5 Clarges St., Piccadilly, London
W1Y 8AB, UK
www.the-kennel-club.org.uk

The Pug is examined by the judge on a table, just like the one you use to groom your dog.

HOW ABOUT AN ILP?

If you have acquired a puppy and have no interest in showing or breeding, you can apply for an ILP or Indefinite Listing Privilege, which affords your dog the opportunity to participate in obedience, agility, tracking and many other performance events. An ILP does not replace the dog's registration certification, and all ILP dogs must belong to an AKC-recognized breed and be spayed or neutered.

judge's ring procedure. If it is your first time in the ring, do not be over-anxious and run to the front of the line. It is much better to stand back and study how the exhibitor in front of you is performing. The judge asks each handler to "stack" the dog, hopefully showing the dog off to his best advantage. The judge will observe the dog from a distance and from different angles, and approach the dog to check his teeth, overall structure, alertness and muscle tone, as well as consider how well the dog "conforms" to the standard. Most importantly, the judge will have the exhibitor move the dog around the ring in some pattern that he should specify (another advantage to not going first, but always listen since some judges change their directions—and the judge is always right!). Finally, the judge

will give the dog one last look before moving on to the next exhibitor.

If you are not in the top four in your class at your first show, do not be discouraged. Be patient and consistent, and you may eventually find yourself in the winning line-up. Remember that the winners were once in your shoes and have devoted many hours and much money to earn the placement. If you find that your dog is losing every time and never getting a nod, it may be time to consider a different dog sport or to just enjoy your Pug as a pet.

OBEDIENCE TRIALS

Obedience trials in the US trace back to the early 1930s when organized obedience training was developed to demonstrate how well dog and owner could work together. The pioneer of obedience trials is Mrs. Helen Whitehouse Walker, a Standard Poodle fancier, who designed a series of exercises after the Associated Sheep, Police Army Dog Society of Great Britain. Since the days of Mrs. Walker, obedience trials have grown by leaps and bounds, and today there are over 2,000 trials held in the US every year, with more than 100,000 dogs competing. Any registered AKC dog can enter an obedience trial, regardless of conformational disqualifications or neutering.

Obedience trials are divided

"Companion Dog." The Open level requires that the dog perform the same exercises as previously mentioned but without a leash for extended lengths of time, as well as retrieve a dumbbell, broad jump and drop on recall. In the Utility level, dogs must perform ten difficult exercises, including scent discrimination, hand signals for basic commands, directed jump and directed retrieve.

The rewards of dog showing are evident in this charming photograph taken after a long and successful day of competing in the ring. Juniors have proven to be marvelous handlers for Pugs and other Toy breeds.

into three levels of progressive difficulty. At the first level, the Novice, dogs compete for the title Companion Dog (CD); at the intermediate level, the Open, dogs compete for the title Companion Dog Excellent (CDX); and at the advanced level, the Utility, dogs compete for the title Utility Dog (UD). Classes are sub-divided into "A" (for beginners) and "B" (for more experienced handlers). A perfect score at any level is 200, and a dog must score 170 or better to earn a "leg," of which three are needed to earn the title. To earn points, the dog must score more than 50% of the available points in each exercise; the possible points range from 20 to 40.

Each level consists of a different set of exercises. In the Novice level, the dog must heel on- and off-lead, come, long sit, long down and stand for examination. These skills are the basic ones required for a well-behaved

INDEX

Page numbers in **boldface** indicate illustrations.

𝕸𝖞 𝕻𝖚𝖌

PUT YOUR PUPPY'S FIRST PICTURE HERE

Dog's Name _____

Date _____ Photographer _____